Downsize This!

Downsize This!

Michael Moore

PAN BOOKS

First published in 1996 by Crown Publishers, Inc., 201 East 50th Street,
New York, New York 10022, USA

First published in Great Britain in 1997 by Boxtree

This edition published 2002 by Pan Books,
an imprint of Pan Macmillan Ltd
Pan Macmillan, 20 New Wharf Road,
London N1 9RR
Basingstoke and Oxford

Associated companies throughout the world

ISBN 0 330 41915 3

19 18 17 16 15 14 13 12 11 10

A CIP catalogue record for this book is available from
the British Library

Printed and bound in Great Britain by Mackays of Chatham plc,
Chatham, Kent

To my wife, Kathleen,
and my daughter, Natalie . . .
two very funny people
I love immensely

Contents

Downsize This!

Oklahoma City, Oklahoma, 1995

Flint, Michigan, 1996

THE ETIQUETTE OF DOWNSIZING

Compiled from various internal memos of companies that are currently downsizing, including Chemical Bank and the Times-Mirror Company, among others.

TERMINATION GUIDELINES

1. The termination meeting should last no more than 5 to 10 minutes.

2. The termination meeting should be held in a neutral location, with easy access for security.

3. Avoid any small talk. Get to the point. Don't debate. Don't discuss any issues of "fairness."

4. The downsized employee should clearly understand that he or she is being *fired* and this will be his or her *last* day of work.

5. Have Kleenex available.

6. Be supportive and empathetic, but not compromising. Use silence to give the employee an opportunity to react to the news.

7. Don't be defensive or argumentative. Don't be apologetic.

8. Don't provide extensive justification for the downsizing decision.

9. Do not try to make light of the situation by making jokes or trying to be funny.

10. Remain calm and try not to display any emotion.

11. If the employee becomes too emotional, suggest that he or she see a counselor. You may need to restate the message that he or she has been fired to ensure that the employee knows that the decision is final and has been made at the highest level for the good of the company.

12. The following are the four most common emotional responses employees have upon learning of their termination and the best way for the manager to handle them:

• **ANGER.** The louder the downsized employee talks, the softer the manager should talk. The idea is to diffuse confrontation, since the employee cannot have a one-sided argument.

• **DENIAL.** Just because a person has been told, "You're fired," does not mean that he or she really hears it or believes it. The manager's role is to let individuals know the importance of getting their lives back together as soon as possible.

• **DEPRESSION.** This type of emotion should send an immediate warning signal. The person should be referred to a human resources counselor.

• **HYSTERIA.** Both men and women are capable of overreacting to news of their termination. For terminated people who begin to cry after hearing the news, have a glass of water handy.

13. The manager who conducts the termination wants to hear a fired employee say, "Can I see you again?" or "How much am I getting in severance?" Such comments show that the downsized individual is getting over the news and thinking about the future.

14. Managers need to recognize the following symptoms during the meeting that may indicate the terminated worker could turn violent: expression of unusual or bizarre thoughts; a fixation on weapons; romantic obsession; depression; and chemical dependence.

15. Request that the employee turn over his or her keys and other property of the company. Secure all access to the computers.

16. Contact security immediately if any assistance is required to escort the terminated employee from the property.

17. Offer the number of any services that may be of help to the terminated individual, such as temporary employment agencies, government assistance programs, out-of-state job banks, and a list of phone numbers for nearby moving services such as U-Haul and Ryder Truck.

Let's All Hop in a
Ryder Truck

SINCE MAKING *Roger & Me* in 1989, I've listened to a lot of stories from people, strangers in the street, who want to buy me a beer or a burger and tell me what happened to their American Dream. *Roger & Me* chronicled how the world's richest corporation, General Motors, destroyed my hometown of Flint, Michigan, by firing 30,000 workers during a time when the company was making record profits. I filmed my search to find the chairman of GM, Roger Smith, and tried to convince him to come to Flint so he could see what he had done to the people there.

Although Roger never made it to Flint, a lot of other people have. These days everyone, it seems, lives in their own Flint, Michigan.

CHAPTER 1

The stories I hear are pretty much the same, with a few variations to allow for the pink-slipped brother who committed suicide, or the mother who lost her life savings when the pension fund went belly-up. I have heard so many of these stories that I can fill in the blanks before the sentences are finished. I find myself doing this to keep from sinking into a deep despair.

It is not pleasant when a homeless person actually *knows* you and calls out, "Hey, Mike!" as you are trying to walk quickly past him and his shopping cart. This happened to me on 46th Street in New York City in front of the Paramount Hotel. I was with a vice president of NBC and the producers of my show "TV Nation." The homeless man grabbed my hand for a shake and told me he, too, was from Flint, Michigan, but now lives here on the street.

He wanted to describe his favorite part of *Roger & Me*, which he had seen three years ago when he had a job. The NBC executive couldn't believe what he was watching. And I'm thinking . . . I know this guy!

"You remember me, don't you?" he asked. "I used to deliver your newspaper, the *Flint Voice*."

Why was it him standing there like that? Why not me? But for the grace of Warner Bros. and NBC? I emptied my pockets and gave him everything I had. We left him on the street and went inside, where I had a $30 steak. The NBC suit had a salad. My buddy from Flint was probably already guzzling his aptly named Colt .45.

• • •

As I write this I am on a plane to Ames, Iowa, to speak to a group of students and farmers who, like the strangers in the street, are angry and depressed that the America they once believed in has all but told them where to get off. When I arrive, the auditorium is overflowing. I begin to hear the same stories of betrayal and bewilderment and, always, the Big Question. Why is it that if they worked so hard for so long, and played by the rules, and voted for the Republicans, their reward has been foreclosure and divorce, bankruptcy and "the bottle"?

As I sit offstage listening to the introduction, I think about how I, too, was raised to believe in an America where everyone had the opportunity to achieve a decent life. I was the all-American boy, an Eagle Scout. I won my Marksman certificate from the NRA. I was religious, attending the seminary in high school to become a Catholic priest. I obeyed all the rules (to this day, I have yet to smoke a joint) and worked within our political system (at the age of eighteen, I was elected to public office in Michigan). Until the 1990s, I never earned more than $15,000 a year. I have stood in the unemployment line at least three different times in my life and was collecting $98 a week in "benefits" when I decided to make *Roger & Me*.

Now, after years of living when I barely had enough money to even go to the movies, I find myself suddenly blessed with the opportunity to *make* them. I feel truly privileged to be able to speak to so many people. But tonight, I can't stop thinking about the two people I met on my way here to Ames.

"Bill" is what the name read on his shirt, as he stood under the big Delta logo (YOU'LL LOVE THE WAY WE FLY) behind the airline counter. He took my ticket, looked at the name, looked up at me (one of those "you look so much thinner on TV" looks), and smiled.

"I just saw your movie for the third time," he said, his face turning red because he thinks he's meeting a movie star or something. "I just want to thank you for what you did."

I thanked him for thanking me and then he told me his story.

"I'm fifty years old. Worked here at Delta for twenty-one

years. Two years ago, they announced they were downsizing the company and told me I was being laid off. I went into shock. Almost twenty years with the company. Where was I going to get a job at fifty years old? They told us they were bringing in outside part-time contractors to do our jobs. Temps. We were welcome to apply for those jobs if we wanted to—at half our former wage. I just couldn't do it."

"So," I interrupted, "how many prescriptions did you eventually go on?"

"Six," he replied, without missing a beat. "Prozac, Xanax, Pepcid, Lasix, Clonidine for my blood pressure . . ."

". . . And something to help you sleep at night."

"Yeah, Ambien, how'd you guess?"

"I get stopped a lot. People who have lost their jobs want to show me their portable pill cases—you know, a little compartment for each day of the week or—"

"Or each pill compartment divided by color," he said, finishing my sentence as he pulled out his plastic medicine chest to show me.

"You're not flying this plane I'm taking, are you?" I asked half-seriously.

He told me that the only way he got to come back to work was because someone had died and he was highest on the seniority list. "I'm down to three pills a day," Bill said, mustering a little pride. "Things are looking up."

• • •

The cabbie on the way to the airport had also seen *Roger & Me*.

"Hey, you're that guy, Roger Moore," he said as he turned around.

"Yeah." I don't tell him my name is Michael. I probably should. Michael Moore, son of Frank and Veronica, brother to Anne and Veronica, no relation to 007.

"I have two master's degrees," he began. "I've been laid off from two different jobs in the last five years. Nobody wants a guy with this much education. So now I'm driving a cab."

"I'm supposed to be in Flint building Buicks," I tell him, "but I quit the day I was to start. Many years ago."

The cabbie glanced at me in the rearview mirror, probably glad I wasn't the one who had built *his* Buick. "I've got a question for you, Mr. Moore. Why is it that Al D'Amato and the rest of Congress have spent TWO YEARS and TEN MIL-LION DOLLARS investigating why seven—*seven*, mind you—SEVEN people lost their jobs in the White House travel office and not a single dime or day has been spent investigating why THIRTY MILLION *other* Americans have lost *their* jobs? WHY IS THAT?"

"I've got a few ideas," I reply, but before I can offer them, he answers the question.

"Because the Big Guys who threw us out of work are the same ones paying these politicians to keep the country distracted with some phony Whitewater issue. Any fool can see that."

• • •

We are a bunch of fools, aren't we? Today, we're actually earning *less* than we earned, in real dollars, in *1979!* Millions of people officially are out of work—7,266,000. But the Bureau of Labor Statistics and the Census Bureau estimate another 5,378,000 are also unemployed but *uncounted*. Another 4,500,000 more are working *part-time* but looking for a full-time job. And then there are the 2,520,000 Americans who are working full-time and earning a wage that is *below the poverty line*.

*That's nearly **20 million** people who cannot make the bare minimum they need to survive!*

Meanwhile, the chief executive officers, the CEOs of our top 300 companies, are earning *212 times* what their average worker is earning. As these CEOs fire thousands of employees, they, in turn, become even wealthier. AT&T chairman Robert Allen lays off 40,000 workers while making $16 million. Louis Gerstner of IBM fires 60,000 workers, then takes home $2.6 million. Scott Paper fires 11,000 people, merges with Kimberly-Clark, and CEO Albert Dunlap bags $100 million!

These corporations then go on to post record profits. And how do they celebrate their success? By firing even more people! General Motors made $34 billion in profits over the past fifteen years—and eliminated over 240,000 jobs.

Yet, with every round of firings, the societal problems we must deal with rise at a corresponding rate. According to a study conducted by economists at the University of Utah, for every 1 percent rise in the jobless rate, homicides increase by 6.7 percent, violent crimes by 3.4 percent, crimes against property go up 2.4 percent, and deaths by heart disease and stroke rise by 5.6 and 3.1 percent, respectively.

No matter how rosy Washington tries to paint the news about the economy ("The lowest rates of unemployment and inflation in years!"), the average American *knows* that the jig is up. No one, these days, can remember what job security used to feel like because everyone lives in total fear that he or she could be next. No one is safe. So you learn not to complain as you are forced to work longer hours for lower pay. Health benefits? Paid vacations? You've already kissed them good-bye.

Remember the American Dream? For those of you too young to have ever experienced it, this is what it used to be:

If you work hard, and your company prospers, you, too, shall prosper.

That dream has gone up in smoke. It has been turned into the American *Bad* Dream:

If you work hard, and the company prospers—you lose your job!

There is no more telling sign about the state of the union than this one simple fact: Manpower, Inc.—the nationwide temp agency—has surpassed General Motors as the number one employer in America. More people now work for a company that guarantees you employment only for a day at a time than the company that once proclaimed "What's good for General Motors is good for the country."

We all know it's over, this way of life we once had, or thought we could have if we did well for ourselves. Now we must fight each other for whatever scraps are left, leaving the rich to enjoy the greatest wealth this country has ever seen.

From the look of things as I've described them, you'd think the whole country would be up in arms over how the well-to-do have gotten away with bloody murder. You would think that we'd have mass political movements organizing the working poor. You would think new political parties would be forming to stop this destruction of the American Dream.

You would think that, but you would be wrong. Instead, the majority of Americans have decided that the best statement they can make is no statement at all. In the 1994 election, more than 60 percent of all voting-age Americans—118,535,278 people, or the equivalent of the voting-age population of 42 states—chose to stay home and *not* participate. They did so not because they are apathetic or ignorant or careless. *They didn't vote because they have had their fill of it.* The candidates and the two political parties no longer have anything to say to the citizens of this country. The Democrats and Republicans are so much alike, obediently supporting the very system that has brought ruin to so many families, that the average American couldn't care less what any of them have to say. They know that *voting* will *not* improve their lives, not one single bit.

It is significant to note that, in the 1992 presidential election, nearly 20 percent of those who did vote actually took the time to drive to the polls and stand in line to cast their ballot for a man most of them knew was a certified fruitcake—Ross Perot. That's how intense the level of anger is in this country. Millions threw away their vote simply because they thought it would send a message! Perot, as nutty as he is, was saying a lot of the things that no one else was saying about the American worker—a real irony considering the billions he owns and the fact that his Democratic opponent, Bill Clinton (raised by a single mother, at times impoverished), said little or nothing.

It is even more surprising that in 1996 a majority of Americans said that if they had the chance, they would elect Colin Powell as president. That these downsized Americans would be able to push through their own personal racism just so they could send a message about how angry they were over their plight was a powerful signal that all is not well in the U.S. of A. Did you ever think things would get this bad in America that you would live to see the day when a majority of white voters pleaded for a *black* guy to run for president? They would never want him to move next door or marry their daughter—but they would put him in the highest office in the land! Wow.

In my home state of Michigan, the situation has sunk so low that only *12 percent* of the voters went to the polls in the March primary, even though at that time there was a bitterly contested race between Bob Dole and Pat Buchanan. Buchanan knew firsthand just how bad things have gotten for the country—in part because he had spent most of his life in the Nixon and Reagan White Houses *making* it bad!

But now he had transformed himself overnight into The Great White Workers' Hope. Like a man who had preceded him on the political scene over sixty years ago (albeit in Germany), Buchanan knew just what to say to the disenfranchised, abused American worker: HATE! FEAR! MORE HATE! BLAME THE IMMIGRANTS!

He almost pulled it off, getting about a third of the Republican vote, even winning a few states. It speaks well of the goodness of the American people that they did not fall for his ruse. It is very easy to manipulate people when they are down on their luck. Very easy to plug in to their psyche with all the "right" answers to "Who did this to you?"

Many citizens, though, are not just sitting idly by watching their country go down the drain. In October 1995, one million African-American men marched on Washington, D.C., to let America know they had had it. It did not matter to most of them that the march was led by a weirdo. What mattered was *making the statement.* And did they. One out of every ten black men in this country found a way to get to Washington, D.C., that day (the equivalent of 8 million white guys holding a demonstration). It made a powerful impression on an already frightened white America.

Just how frightened is evidenced by the growing militia movement. Tens of thousands of men and women are training, with weapons, for what they believe will be the ultimate confrontation with the government. Although most of them are motivated by racist beliefs, a lot of their sympathizers are just the average Joes who live next door to *you.* But not for long. The bank has foreclosed on their house and repossessed their car and the money they had put away to send the kids to college is now used to buy food, clothes, and maybe someday a few semi-automatic weapons. They have, in essence, snapped. It's one thing to have always been poor and never possessed those niceties of middle-class life. It's a whole 'nother thing to have enjoyed those privileges and then have them taken away from you—by the very people you voted for!

When that happens, many individuals who are already on the edge and can't figure out how to respond politically are going to do one of two things: (a) Take it out on themselves (sit in the dark and drink), or (b) Take it out on *you*. In Michigan alone, the birthplace of downsizing, there are over fifty militia groups, the most in the country.

• • •

My parents called yesterday to tell me that GM has announced two more plant closings in Flint (are there any left to close?). Another 3,000 lives will be torn apart.

Many of these people who will lose their jobs are recent arrivals from Oklahoma City. They moved to Flint (a few months after the bombing of their federal building) when GM closed a factory there and told the workers with higher seniority that they could relocate to Flint if they chose. So they rented their Ryder trucks and headed to Michigan with the promise of the company that they would be secure (in Flint!). Now, nine months later, they will be forced to call Ryder Truck and move again. They've been told this time that they can go to Lansing.

• • •

What is terrorism? There is no question that, when an individual rents a Ryder Truck, loads it with explosives, and blows up a building, it is an act of terrorism and should be severely punished.

But what do you call it when a *company* destroys the lives of thousands of people? Is this terrorism? *Economic* terrorism? The company doesn't use a homemade bomb or a gun. They systematically move out all of the people before they blow up the building. But as I pass by the remnants of that factory there in Flint, Michigan, looking eerily like the remnants of the Alfred P. Murrah Federal Building in Oklahoma City, I wonder: What will happen to *those* people? A few will kill themselves, despondent over the loss of their livelihood. Some will be killed by their spouse—an argument over the lack of a new job or the loss of money at the racetrack turns suddenly violent (the woman is the one who usually ends up dead). Others will be killed more slowly through drugs or alcohol, the substances of choice when one needs to ease the pain of his or her life being turned upside down and shoved into an empty, dark hole.

We don't call the company a murderer, and we certainly don't call their actions terrorism, but make no mistake about it, their victims will be just as dead as those poor souls in Oklahoma City, killed off in the name of greed.

There is a rage building throughout the country and, if you're like me, you're scared shitless. Oklahoma City is the extreme extension of this rage. Though most people are somehow able to keep their wits through these hard times, I believe thousands of Americans are only a few figurative steps away from getting into that Ryder Truck. How terrifyingly ironic that the vehicle now chosen for terrorist acts is the same one used by that vast diaspora of working-class Americans who have spent the last decade moving from state to state in the hopes of survival.

This moving van, this symbol of their downsized lives, has become a means to an end. Eighty pounds of fertilizer and a fuse made of ammonium nitrate and fuel oil now fill the trusty Ryder instead of the kids' bunk beds and the dining room set.

Timothy McVeigh couldn't get a decent job in Buffalo, so he joined the army and got the "first kill" of his unit in Iraq during the Gulf War. He was praised and rewarded. The next year, he was unemployed, hanging around Niagara Falls, New York. A photo of him that has been widely published shows him and fellow defendant Terry Nichols horsing around on the ledge at Niagara Falls. I was there at the Falls, writing and prepping my film *Canadian Bacon,* at the time that photo was taken. I, of course, have no recollection of seeing McVeigh there, because who was he then? Just another son of a GM worker who couldn't get a job, not even as a toll-taker on the bridge to Canada (he had scored second highest on the test; there just weren't any openings). In the first scene we filmed a few months later at the Falls, the character Roy-Boy is a laid-off worker (also a veteran of the Gulf War) and is on that same ledge, preparing to jump and end it all.

How was it that Timothy McVeigh became so confused and filled with so much anger? What struck me most about his alleged act was that he had decided to *kill his own people* to make his point. This was a strange twist for those on the extreme Right who had always used their violence against blacks, Jews, and immigrants. But McVeigh is not accused of taking that Ryder Truck to the place where his "enemies" were—the Capitol Building, the World Trade Center, a Jewish temple, the headquarters of the NAACP, or other potential targets of his hate. No. He blows up his own people! In mostly white, Christian conservative, Republican-voting, redneck-lovin' Oklahoma City! Talk about the final insanity.

I do not like guns. I am a pacifist at heart. As a member of that minority of Americans who are unarmed, I have to find another way to combat the downsizing tide that seems to be rising against us. So I have written this book. I have no college degree, so take what I say with that in mind. I'm not even supposed to be writing this book right now, because

I'm under contract to produce a sitcom I've been hired to write for Fox. A sitcom! Hell, I still owe Mr. Rickets an English paper from twelfth-grade Shakespeare! How did I ever get here from Flint?

Oh, yeah. In a Ryder Truck.

Would Pat Buchanan Take a Check from Satan?

POLITICIANS, AS WE all know, will take a campaign contribution from wherever they can get it. But will they really take a check from just anyone? Sure, corporate money controls our elections, that's no big news. A business couldn't care less about what party a candidate belongs to, just as long as the politician will do its bidding. That's why a company like RJR Nabisco has given over a million dollars to Republicans and another half-million to Democrats in the last few years. The only party RJR Nabisco belongs to is the RJR Nabisco party. And the candidates don't really worry about the deadly tobacco products RJR Reynolds pushes; they just want the money.

But I got to thinking—am I being too cynical about our political system? Would the good men and women who hold office actually accept a contribution

CHAPTER 2

from a group they found repulsive, reprehensible, opposed to their stated beliefs? Remember earlier in the campaign when Bob Dole received a check from the Log Cabin Republicans? When Dole learned what those Republicans were doing in those "log cabins" (they were all gay), he returned the check. But then he had a change of heart, thinking, hey, wait a minute, I NEED THE MONEY! So he apologized to the Log Cabiners and blamed the whole thing on his staff.

When it comes to campaign money, there can be no hate. To prove my point, I decided to try an experiment. During the early stages of the 1996 presidential contest, I formed several legal organizations. I then sent a number of checks to the leading candidates, as well as to Ross Perot, just to see how greedy they could be. I appointed my assistant, Gillian, the head of each organization and the signatory of each check.

Legitimate $75 and $100 checks went to all the candidates from the following organizations:

- Pedophiles for Free Trade
- The John Wayne Gacey Fan Club
- Hemp Growers of America
- Satan Worshipers for Dole
- Abortionists for Buchanan

What was the response? The Dole campaign returned two checks from Satan Worshipers for Dole. The John Wayne Gacey Fan Club's donation to Perot was returned with a nice letter saying, "We appreciate your generous support and will contact you once the party is established in your state."

But there was one candidate who was not ashamed to take money from anyone, regardless how repulsive he thinks that group may be.

The candidate was Pat Buchanan. And these are the checks he cashed.

You would think that the most strident ideologue of all, Patrick Buchanan, would be the last one to accept money from a group of pro-abortionists and a fan club for a vicious serial killer. But there's the rub with Pat Buchanan.

He doesn't really believe in anything except himself. He's changed his positions so many times, I'm surprised few journalists have called him on it. When I appeared on "Crossfire" with him a few years ago, he was a rabid supporter of Corporate America and demeaned all the people who complained about losing their jobs. Then suddenly, last year, the guy is standing in front of closed factories declaring himself the Working Man's Hero.

So it is a pleasure to see Pat cash these checks—and even more gratifyingly ironic when you consider that this little experiment was actually *his* idea some twenty-five years ago.

In 1972 Buchanan, then working for President Nixon, proposed smearing Nixon challenger Representative Pete McCloskey (an antiwar Republican running for president) by arranging donations to McCloskey's campaign from "Gay Liberation and/or Black Panthers and/or Students for a Democratic Society [SDS]." He then proposed that the donations be leaked to the press. Buchanan wrote to White House chief of staff H. R. Haldeman in a confidential memo dated December 15, 1971:

> *And when the check [is] cashed, that fact [could be] brought to the attention of the voters of New Hampshire . . . who might be skeptical of the source of the funds. . . . [Our mission is to] paint McCloskey as a Democratic tool, and destroy his credibility as a legitimate Republican.*

Buchanan urged that they try to find anything linking McCloskey to "peace money, New York Jewish money and California fat cat money." This memo can be found in the National Archives in the Buchanan file of the Nixon White House papers.

To date, Pat has yet to cash the check we sent him from the Satan Worshipers for Dole club. Maybe there is still time to save his soul.

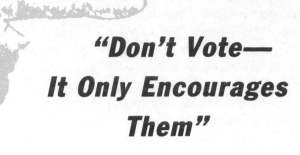

"Don't Vote—
It Only Encourages
Them"

MAYBE THE REASON the majority of Americans don't vote is that they're tired of having to choose between Tweedledum and Tweedledumber. The choices are always so pathetic, aren't they? If you went to a restaurant and the waiter told you, "We're sorry, but the only choices we have left on the menu are cottage cheese and fried breadsticks," you'd leave. Nobody would think you were crazy, lazy, apathetic, or not hungry. In fact, imagine this was the only restaurant in town and there was nowhere else to eat. You'd be desperate to find someplace that had what you wanted.

CHAPTER 3

Our American political system is like that restaurant. Most citizens don't vote—not because they're not hungry to participate, but because they've shown up and there's nothing but crap left on the menu. Because it is almost impossible for a third party to make it on the ballot and get proper media coverage, the voter has nowhere else to go. If the voter does decide to go to the polls, there's always that empty feeling in the gut. Who among us marches proudly into the voting booth thinking, I can't wait to vote for these great men and women of vision!

No. Year after year, we drag our ass into some smelly elementary school gym and vote for "the evil of two lessers."

My friend Al once told me one part of the philosophy by which he lives: "Don't vote—it only encourages them." How many times has the candidate you voted for turned around and done the opposite of what he or she promised? Conservatives voted for Nixon and then he turned around and gave them affirmative action. Liberals voted for Clinton and then, when he took office, he started eliminating affirmative action. There are 1,001 other examples of this. It's happened so many times, it's probably why most of you have given up.

In the meantime, everybody's wages are frozen, none of us get home from work before 8:00 P.M., we pray we don't get sick 'cause we can't afford to, and the bank just sent us another thirty-dollar overdraft charge because there wasn't enough money in our account to cover the phone bill.

There's got to be a better way than every four years having to sit through two boring conventions, smarmy political TV ads, and the ever-dull League of Women Voters debates. All this valuable airtime is devoted to an activity that over a hundred million Americans *don't even participate in!* More people go to horse and dog races in this country than vote. Why don't we see a bunch of greyhounds chasing a little rabbit down the track on prime-time television? I have never seen David Brinkley call the play-by-play from Churchill Downs. Why not? It's what America really wants!

This gives me an idea. If the politicians really want to get more people interested in the election, maybe they should be forced to participate in some real contests—different kinds of races that would test their mettle far better than answering inane questions from Bernard Shaw. Imagine replacing the primaries and the general election with presidential contests that would really get everybody excited and involved in the campaign.

I propose we do away with these meaningless elections and replace them with real races between the candidates that will give us a clear-cut winner. Any of the following contests for the next presidential election in the year 2000 will be far better than what we have now.

NEW, IMPROVED WAYS TO PICK A PRESIDENT

1. Monster Truck Race. The two presidential candidates compete head-on in a couple of trucks with huge, oversized wheels. Imagine how many Americans would tune in if Dole was behind the wheel of "Bigfoot" and Clinton was driving "King Kong." The winner gets to be president. Easy, simple, and over in a matter of minutes.

2. Magic Contest. David Copperfield puts each of the candidates in a straitjacket, places them in separate locked boxes, and dumps them into San Francisco Bay. The first one to wriggle out and come to the surface gets to sit in the Oval Office in January. The loser gets the full ceremony at Arlington, including the 21-gun salute and an eternal flame.

3. SAT. Each candidate is put in a room full of high school juniors and is forced to retake his SAT test. The one with the highest score hears "Hail to the Chief" on January 20. Low scorer must enroll in Hooked on Phonics and is prohibited from running for any other elective office for at least six years.

4. Gender Gap. Each candidate must name a female vice-presidential running mate. He who wins the election must then shoot himself. This isn't really a contest, just a point. It appears a guy would have to get shot before we ever see a woman president.

5. American Gladiators. Clinton and Dole try to knock each other off a Velcro wall. What other country could boast such an event?

6. Cheers. Each candidate will step up to the bar and down twenty shots of tequila (worm optional). First one to recite the Bill of Rights while balancing the shot glass on his nose wins.

7. Run with the Bulls. Bill and Bob go to Pamplona, Spain, and run with the bulls. The first one to cross the line with all his body parts is the new president. Sponsored by the Beef Council of America.

8. Tough-Man Contest. A no-holds-barred kickboxing extravaganza. A fight to the death. Audience encouraged not to cheer for both to lose.

9. Drive-by Shooting Contest. With semiautomatic weapons. The candidates drive by each other's headquarters and spray the place with bullets. The one with the most staff still standing wins.

10. Shock Jock Call-ins. Clinton and Dole are forced to appear on every local shock jock morning show in the country. They must sit there in the nude, describe each other's "shortcomings," and make prank calls to girls who wouldn't date them in high school. Each morning we'll take the tenth caller and let that person vote. At the end of the tour, those votes are tallied and the winner becomes President of the United States of America.

• • •

Sounds like fun, eh? I'll bet turning the presidential election into any of the above races would guarantee more than the usual 40 percent turnout. So let's skip the campaigning, forget about the attack ads, and for crying out loud, no more preempting "Seinfeld" to carry a debate featuring two white guys in blue suits pretending to be enemies when in fact they believe in most of the same things!

Democrat? Republican? Can You Tell the Difference?

CHAPTER 4

THEY CALL THEMSELVES Democrats and Republicans. But you know better. They're really two sides of the same coin!

They act alike, they walk alike, at times they even talk alike—it will blow your mind—our two parties, they're one of a kind. They're the Republicrats! Proud sponsors of our one-party political system—the one *you* don't bother participating in because . . . what's the use? As hard as they try to sound different, they just can't help sounding alike.

Feeling confused? Take the Republicrat's Quiz. Sort out the poseurs from the impostors! Sharpen your pencils, and here we go!

PART I: MULTIPLE CHOICE

Who said the following—a Democrat or a Republican?

1. "I have always supported voluntary prayer in the schools. . . . We can't renew our country unless more of us—I mean all of us—are willing to join churches."

    A. The Reverend Jerry Falwell, Republican
    B. Bill Clinton, Democrat
    C. Oliver North, Republican
    D. The Reverend Jesse Jackson, Democrat

    Answer: B—Bill Clinton, Democrat, in a November 1994 press conference in Indonesia, and in his 1994 State of the Union Address.

2. "We've reached the point that we need the discipline of a balanced budget amendment."

    A. Ronald Reagan, Republican
    B. George Bush, Republican
    C. Senator Robert Dole, Republican
    D. Senator Paul Simon, Democrat

    Answer: D—Senator Paul Simon, Democrat, in a February 23, 1995, press release applauding Senator Tom Harkin's (D-Iowa) decision to vote for the balanced budget amendment.

3. "Performance artists in a free society have the right to do the most extraordinary and bizarre things. That's called 'Freedom of Speech.'"

    A. Newt Gingrich, Republican
    B. Tom Hayden, Democrat
    C. Pat Robertson, Republican
    D. Jerry Brown, Democrat

Answer: A—Newt Gingrich, Republican, in a breakfast meeting with reporters in January 1995.

4. "Participate in tree-planting programs. Take part in special environment events, including commemorating Earth Day and Arbor Day. Adopt a highway, walking trail, or bike path. Become an active member of local conservation groups and boards. Initiate recycling programs. Hand out tree saplings."

    A. Al Gore, Democrat
    B. Fleetwood Mac, Democrats
    C. Lady Bird Johnson, Democrat
    D. A position paper from the House Republican Conference

Answer: D—The House Republican Conference.

5. "There is no health care crisis in America."

    A. Senator Daniel Patrick Moynihan, Democrat
    B. Senator Robert Dole, Republican
    C. Ninety-three-year-old Senator Strom Thurmond, Republican
    D. Dr. Jack Kevorkian (party affiliation unknown)

Answer: A tie! A and B—Senators Moynihan, Democrat, on "Meet the Press" (January 1994) and Dole, Republican, in remarks to reporters (December 1993).

PART II: TRUE OR FALSE

1. The rate of deficit spending was higher under Clinton than under Reagan or Bush. TRUE or FALSE?

Answer: False. Under Reagan and Bush, deficit spending was 5 percent of the gross domestic product (GDP). Under

Clinton's first two budgets, deficit spending dropped to 2.5 percent of the GDP.

2. The warmongering Republicans were responsible for the Korean and Vietnam wars. The Democrats are the party of peace. TRUE or FALSE?

> *Answer: False. Democrats were in the White House when the United States sent troops to fight in Korea and Vietnam. Total U.S. deaths: 112,185. Goals accomplished: None.*

3. The Democrats were responsible for enforcing the first antiabortion restrictions after *Roe v. Wade*. TRUE or FALSE?

> *Answer: True. In 1977, Jimmy Carter signed the law prohibiting Medicaid-funded abortions for poor women.*

4. The federal deficit has grown during the Clinton presidency. TRUE or FALSE?

> *Answer: False. The deficit exceeded $300 billion a year five times during the Reagan-Bush years. When Clinton was elected president, the federal budget deficit was $290 billion. In 1995, the deficit was down to $163.8 billion.*

5. Four out of the five Democratic women senators voted in favor of the Republican welfare bill in 1995, which officially reversed the Democratic Party's sixty-year commitment to a federal safety net for the poor. TRUE or FALSE?

> *Answer: True. Senators Barbara Mikulski (Maryland), Dianne Feinstein (California), Barbara Boxer (California), and Patty Murray (Washington) voted for the Republican bill. Only Senator Carol Moseley-Braun (Illinois) voted no.*

PART III: WHO SAID WHAT?

The speakers are:

A. Governor George W. Bush Jr. of Texas, Republican
B. Senator Edward Kennedy of Massachusetts, Democrat
C. Speaker of the House Newt Gingrich of Georgia, Republican

Match the speaker to the quote:

1. "[We] need to end the abuses in the current immigration laws that jeopardize the jobs of American workers. At stake are hundreds of thousands of good jobs that should be available to *American* workers!"

> *Answer: B—Senator Kennedy, Democrat, in a news conference on February 12, 1996.*

2. "We should be as open and enthusiastic as ever about people who want to enter America as legal immigrants."

> *Answer: C—Representative Gingrich, Republican, in his book* To Renew America.

3. "We will tolerate no bashing of Mexico or immigrants. Candidates who bash immigrants will be asked to pay the price."

> *Answer: A—Governor Bush, Republican, in El Paso, Texas, on August 11, 1995.*

PART IV: WHO'S YOUR HERO?

Newt Gingrich and Bill Clinton greatly admire past leaders. Which one said the following:

1. "The greatest leaders in fighting for an integrated America in the twentieth century were in the Democratic Party. The fact is, it was the liberal wing of the Democratic Party that ended segregation. The fact is, it was Franklin Roosevelt who gave hope to a nation that was in despair."

   A. Bill Clinton
   B. Newt Gingrich

   Answer: B—Newt Gingrich, Republican, in his acceptance speech as Speaker of the House, January 5, 1995.

2. "I was struck by the rigor of [President Nixon's] analysis and the wisdom of his suggestions. President Nixon believed deeply that the United States cannot be strong at home unless we lead abroad."

   A. Bill Clinton
   B. Newt Gingrich

   Answer: A—Bill Clinton, Democrat, in an address to the Nixon Center for Peace and Freedom, March 1995.

3. "To Ronald Reagan, whom we wish well tonight, who exhorted us to carry on until the twilight struggle against communism was won."

   A. Bill Clinton
   B. Newt Gingrich

   Answer: A—Bill Clinton, Democrat, in his 1995 State of the Union Address.

4. "I want a government that is smaller and less bureaucratic. We have given you the smallest government, not the other party . . . in thirty years, and the biggest reduction in regulations."

A. Bill Clinton
B. Newt Gingrich

Answer: A—Bill Clinton, Democrat, in remarks to the Ohio Democrats, March 1996.

PART V: BONUS QUESTION

Who said: "We wanted the Power Rangers here because they're multiethnic role models in which women and men play equally strong roles"?

A. Michael Eisner
B. Big Bird
C. Hillary Clinton
D. Newt Gingrich

Answer: That's right, D—Republican Newt, at a children's party on Capitol Hill for kids whose parents are House Republicans, January 1995.

• • •

Congratulations! You've completed the quiz. If you scored less than 50 percent and decide not to vote on Election Day, we'll understand.

> "I think God made all people good. But if we had to take a million immigrants in—say, Zulus next year, or Englishmen—and put them in Virginia, what group would be easier to assimilate and would cause less problems for the people of Virginia?"
>
> —Pat Buchanan

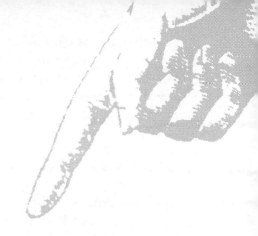

Not on the Mayflower? Then Leave!

C H A P T E R 5

I'M SURE IT'S just a coincidence that one of my fantasies has always been to see Pat Buchanan assimilating with a bunch of Zulus. So, yes, Pat, I would like to have a million Zulus move into your Virginia neighborhood. In fact, unlike you, I have a very simple immigration policy for the entire country: let everyone in except bigots like you.

If you're a Buchanan lover, I guess that means pack your bags, too. I suppose you don't find it the least bit hypocritical to believe immigrants should not be allowed into America when none of us would be here unless our great-grandparents hadn't somehow finagled *their* way in. Other than African Americans (who were forcibly brought here) or Native American Indians (who came here first), the rest of us are the result of some pretty risky, tricky, and lucky work by our forefathers and -mothers.

Instead of being grateful for what they did—and for the benefits *we've* reaped because of their actions—many of you now want to exclude others who want to come to America. You've become the same assholes who tried to keep our families out—and made life miserable for them once they arrived.

Immigrants have always been the scapegoats. To hear Pat Buchanan and his ilk describe it, illegal aliens are the cause of our unemployment, they drain our social services, they cause the crime rate to go up, and, worst of all, we can't understand a damn thing they say when they talk.

Of course, the truth is immigrants often work harder than anyone. They don't drain the welfare pool because many of them are afraid even to apply for fear of being caught. And the U.S. crime rate has been falling steadily since 1991—at a time when the number of illegal foreigners has been increasing by 300,000 a year.

These "illegals" are more than willing to do the jobs the rest of us don't want to do, the dirty, backbreaking work—from laboring in the farm fields to cleaning up the mess we've left behind in our hotel room. And what do they get in return? A bunch of complaining from us that we can't understand what they've said in their broken English at the McDonald's take-out window. Maybe Pat Buchanan should work there. *Then we could all get our burger orders right the first time!*

No, you don't want to do that, do you, Pat? God intended something better for *you*—the best school, the good job, the big house, the compliant spouse, and the courtside seats to the rest of life. You want *someone else* to wipe up after you, wash your dishes, and scrub the gum off the floor in your building.

Yet—and here's the part I don't get—you don't want to let *them* into the country to do this dirty work for you. Well, you can't have it both ways. If you insist that everyone residing in America must be a citizen by birth, then I suggest you get down on your hands and knees and wipe the crusted urine off the rim of the office toilet seat yourself.

Why do *I* need to give *you* a lesson in capitalism? Immigrants, legal or illegal, work hard for their money, and they become *consumers* and thus help to *create jobs*. It has struck me as quite odd that right-wingers don't see how this benefits their corrupt system. Capitalists thrive on exploiting labor—and what better group to exploit than a bunch of undocumented Mexicans or Chinese?

For years, that was indeed the sad, sick policy. The INS turned its head and ignored all the illegals because we needed cheap labor. But now that we've downsized half the country, we've got all the cheap, homegrown labor we need!

During the seventies and eighties, the U.S. government was more than willing to let in anyone from Cuba or the former South Vietnam. Why? Because those foreigners were rabid anticommunists and guaranteed Republican voters. Over half a million Cubans have been greeted with open arms as "political refugees" since Castro took over. Here's how it was before Castro: only *three* Cubans were let into the United States as political refugees during the 1940s, and a whopping total of *six* were let in throughout the 1950s when the dictator Batista ruled with an iron fist.

Everyone else for the past half century, whether it was boatloads of Jews trying to escape the Holocaust, or Salvadoran peasants on the run from the death squads, was persona non Americana. No matter what suffering these illegals were experiencing back home—especially political repression—the Statue of Liberty was not shining for them.

For those of you who continue to demand that we keep the gates closed, let me ask you this: What gives you that right? Unless you are a Native American, you cannot rightfully claim to belong here.

Because I'm in a generous mood, I'll even grant the nutty zealots who were escaping religious persecution on the *Mayflower* special designation as honorary original Americans. Actually, here is a list of passengers from the manifest of the *Mayflower*. If your name isn't among these, ask yourself just how the hell you and yours got here, and by what right *you* deserve to stay.

NAMES OF THOSE ON THE *MAYFLOWER*
(as kept by Christopher Jones, Master, A.D. 1620)

ALDEN	COOPER	LANGMORE	SOULE
ALLERTON	CRACKSTON	LATHAM	STANDISH
BILLINGTON	DOTY	LESTER	STORY
BRADFORD	EATON	MARGESSON	THOMPSON
BREWSTER	ENGLISH	MARTIN	TILLEY
BRITTERIDGE	FLETCHER	MINTER	TINKER
BROWNE	FULLER	MORE	TREVOR
BUTTON	GARDINER	MULLINS	TURNER
CARTER	GOODMAN	PRIEST	WARREN
CARVER	HOLBECK	PROWER	WHITE
CHILTON	HOOKE	RIGDALE	WILDER
CLARKE	HOPKINS	ROGERS	WILLIAMS
COOKE	HOWLAND	SAMPSON	WINSLOW

Not on the list? Then shut the fuck up! Pat Buchanan, if you keep trashing illegal aliens, I swear I'm going to conduct an investigation and find out just how your relatives connived their way into the United States. Why don't you just move on to some other bigoted subject?

Back to the list—it looks like *I'm* on it! I know, there's an "ó" missing from "More," but that probably got dropped when my Irish ancestors illegally immigrated to England before illegally immigrating here.

My immigration policy is simple. Every New Year's Day, we open up the gates and the first hundred thousand people to get in the country, by any means necessary, stay. And the first fifty of that group will receive a free Tipper Gore T-shirt. We will give them their documents and support them in their efforts to become U.S. citizens. Listen, we've got *a lot* of room here. Have you ever driven through Kansas? Man, it seems like it's never going to end! There's plenty of room there for our new Americans. Or how about west Texas? You could go there for a week and never see anyone. We've got lots of space. Montana! Alaska! Downtown Detroit! Let's fill it up with people who actually, unlike many of us, WANT to be here!

For all the talk about how we are infiltrated with more immigrants than any other place in the world, consider these statistics: 22.7 percent of Australia's population is foreign-born. In Switzerland, it's 18.5 percent. Canada's is 16.1 percent. Only 8.7 percent of the United States is made up of people from a foreign land.

In the interests of helping those of you who want to come to America, I've written up a few useful tips for sneaking into the country. Be sure to take these pages with you on your journey—and stop by to see me in New York for coffee, doughnuts, and a complimentary Statue of Liberty key chain.

WAYS TO GET INTO THE UNITED STATES

1. By air. Why is it that we spend millions of dollars patrolling the Mexican border, when more than half of this country's illegal immigrants arrive here by plane? If you decide to sneak in via air, remember that you no longer have to use just the big (and heavily policed) airports like Kennedy and LAX. Now every city in the country has changed the name of its airport to include the word *International*. Yes, there's a Chattanooga International Airport, a Reno International Airport, even an "International" airport in Flint, Michigan. Many of these have their own customs stations—and they are not staffed by the most vigilant residents of their communities. So, if you can afford to, fly to one of these locations, say you're a tourist or a student, and never leave!

2. From Mexico. If you're coming from Mexico, stay away from those border crossings where presidential candidates go to have their pictures taken. A lot of manpower has been invested in these areas to create the illusion of an aggressive anti-immigration policy. Try crossing the Rio Grande near Brownsville, where it is nothing more than a drainage ditch. In Los Ebanos, Texas, there's a little barge that is pulled across the river by a rope, and there you will be greeted by an INS guy who would rather be fishing, so he'll whisk you straight through customs.

3. From Canada. Canada is a great place from which to enter the United States. If you're coming from Europe, fly to Toronto or Montreal, tell the friendly Canadian customs people you've come to see Niagara Falls, and then make your way to the U.S. border. There is virtually no border surveillance between Quebec and Vermont. A good crossing point is the field next to the McDonald's on New York's Route 87, near the Vermont border. Cross over into Vermont right away (less border patrol than in New York), and head down I-89 to exit 10 and then north on Route 100 to Waterbury, where you can visit the home of Ben & Jerry's Ice Cream. Tours take place every thirty minutes, seven days a week, 9:00 A.M. to 5:00 P.M. Be sure to sample the Chocolate Chip Cookie Dough and the Cherry Garcia!

If you really *do* want to visit Niagara Falls, use the middle bridge by the whirlpool in the river, where the INS is a little more lax. Be sure to say that you are going over to shop at the Tops supermarket, where all the Canadians go to get cheap cigarettes and beer. If you want, you can get back into Canada and stay there—something I would personally recommend because you get all the amenities of America in Canada without any of the 23,000 annual murders, and none of the stupidity. Don't worry when you see a Canadian slopping vinegar all over his french fries—they've got free health care! Memorize the phone number for Pizza Pizza, their national pizza chain. If you can say 967-11-11 to the Canadian customs people, they'll think you're Canadian and wave you on in.

If you want to come to my home state of Michigan (the one on the map that looks like a mitten), the best crossing point from Canada is the Bluewater Bridge in Port Huron. I have a fond memory of being strip-searched there during the Vietnam War. But don't worry—they'll let you in. They just like a little peek.

4. By sea. Can you name the country closest in proximity to our southern border after Mexico? That's right, it's Bimini! Barely fifty miles off the Florida coast and made famous by the boat ride Gary Hart took there with Donna Rice, Bimini is very easy to move in and out of. I've been told you can be dropped off secretly by boat in Florida for a hefty $950 (ask for "Lou" on the lower dock), or hop a ride to Miami on the seaplane for $156 plus tax (documents may be checked). Don't try to jet-ski to Florida, because the gas tank will hit empty ten miles out to sea.

5. From Russia. There is one place you can enter the United States and *never* have to worry about seeing the border patrol. The Diomede Islands, in the Bering Strait, have no INS checkpoints. Yet, in the winter, the sea is a frozen slab and you can simply walk from Russia to the United States. This is a perfect route for anyone coming from Asia. Just make your way north through Siberia to Big Diomede Island. Then carefully step across the floating blocks of ice approximately 2.5 miles to the American island of Little Diomede. You will be greeted by friendly Eskimos who will keep you warm and show you the way to the lower forty-eight.

Okay, there are a few drawbacks. First, it's pretty damn cold, so dress warmly. At times the wind gusts up to seventy miles an hour, and visibility is zero. And there is the small matter of polar bears. They are big and nasty and will eat you, green card or no green card. A large rifle in your bag is not a bad idea.

Although this route seems the most difficult, think of the symbolism of your accomplishment. This is the exact path the first "Indians" took from Asia when they came to this land. It is, in essence, the only official, approved, time-tested entrance. Everything after that involved our ancestors barging into places where they weren't welcome.

THEY WALK AMONG US

The following people were not born here. They came to the United States as aliens. Aren't we a better country with them?

MADELEINE ALBRIGHT, *U.S. ambassador to the UN* (Czechoslovakia)

MARIO ANDRETTI, *race-car driver* (Italy)

ANN-MARGRET, *actress/singer* (Sweden)

CLIVE BARNES, *theater critic,* New York Post (England)

SAUL BELLOW, *author* (Canada)

DAVID BYRNE, *musician, Talking Heads* (Scotland)

JOSÉ CANSECO, *baseball star* (Cuba)

LIZ CLAIBORNE, *fashion designer* (Belgium)

GLORIA ESTEFAN, *singer* (Cuba)

PATRICK EWING, *basketball star* (Jamaica)

MAX FRANKEL, *executive editor,* The New York Times (Germany)

TERRY GEORGE, *screenwriter,* In the Name of the Father (Northern Ireland)

PETER JENNINGS, *network anchor* (Canada)

TED KOPPEL, *"Nightline" anchor* (England)

ANGELA LANSBURY, *actress* (England)

YO-YO MA, *cellist* (France)

PETER MAX, *artist* (Germany)

ZUBIN MEHTA, *conductor* (India)

MARTINA NAVRATILOVA, *tennis star* (Czechoslovakia)

MIKE NICHOLS, *director of* The Graduate, The Birdcage (Germany)

HAKEEM OLAJUWON, *basketball star* (Nigeria)

FRANK OZ, *puppeteer and film director* (England)

I. M. PEI, *architect* (China)

ITZHAK PERLMAN, *classical musician* (Israel)

SIDNEY POITIER, *actor* (Bahamas)

ANTHONY QUINN, *actor* (Mexico)

CARLOS SANTANA, *rock musician, Santana* (Mexico)

GENERAL JOHN SHALIKASHVILI, *Chair, Joint Chiefs of Staff* (Poland)

GENE SIMMONS, *rock musician, Kiss* (Israel)

ELIZABETH TAYLOR, *actress* (England)

ALEX TROTMAN, *CEO, Ford Motor Company* (Scotland)

EDDIE VAN HALEN, *rock musician, Van Halen* (the Netherlands)

ELIE WIESEL, *author* (Romania)

BILLY WILDER, *director of* Some Like It Hot (Austria)

NEIL YOUNG, *rock legend* (Canada)

Big Welfare Mamas

I HATE WELFARE mothers. Lazy, shiftless, always trying to get something for nothing. They expect the rest of us to take care of them instead of getting off their collective ass and taking care of themselves. Always looking for a handout, they simply expect us average, hardworking, decent taxpayers to underwrite their illicit behavior as they churn 'em out, one after the other.

How long are we going to tolerate Big Business acting this way?

Each year, freeloading corporations grab nearly $170 billion in tax-funded federal handouts to help them do the things they should be paying for themselves (and that doesn't even count all the corporate welfare they're getting from state and local governments). That's $1,388 from each of us going to provide welfare to the rich!

By contrast, all of our social programs combined, from Aid to Families with Dependent Children (AFDC) to school lunches to housing assistance, amount to just $50 billion a year. That breaks down to only $1.14 a day from each of us.

So why is it that when we say the word *welfare*, the first image that comes to mind is the single mother with a half-dozen kids living in the inner city? Aside from the fact that it's racist, it also isn't true. According to the U.S. government, the majority of welfare recipients are white, live in the suburbs, have two kids, want to work, and stay on welfare an average of only two years. These people, down on their luck, deserve whatever help and respect we can give them.

It's easy to get all worked up about a mythical bunch of "cheaters" and "chiselers" out there taking us for a ride. Especially during these times when we're all so scared about making our own house payment, it doesn't seem to take a whole lot of convincing to turn us against the less fortunate in our society.

Maybe we should be directing our anger elsewhere—like toward Wall Street. Why is it we never think of Big Business when we think of welfare recipients? Companies take more of our tax dollars, and in much more questionable ways, than do those who are trying to heat their apartments with a kerosene stove.

This "ADC"—Aid to Dependent *Corporations*—comes in many forms. Much of it is just outright cash. Other ADC opportunities come by way of generous tax breaks and exemptions that you and I do not get. Still more welfare is dished out through governmental goods and services at low or no cost. And, trust me, it ain't surplus rancid cheese these guys are having to stand in line for once a month.

- It's $1.6 million in federal funds for McDonald's, in part to help them market Chicken McNuggets in Singapore from 1986 to 1994.

to the government to pay for it. In fact, Martin Marietta sought to receive $940,000 in welfare payments for several private company concerts, including Barbara Mandrell, the Righteous Brothers, Gladys Knight, the Temptations, the Beach Boys, Stephanie Mills, and the Ice Capades. But after considerable public pressure, they withdrew this welfare request.

But that doesn't mean Lockheed and Martin Marietta didn't go back to the federal trough. Other welfare payments include:

- $1 billion to cover the cost of plant shutdowns and relocations;

- A $330 million reward from the federal government for acquiring a GE defense subsidiary;

- $2,594,385 in "foreign sales awards" since 1993 for weapons that Lockheed has sold to other countries (these were subsidized in part by the taxpayers, according to the National Commission for Economic Conversion and Disarmament);

- $20,194 for golf balls for Marietta executives;

- $7,589 for the office Christmas party in Oak Ridge, Tennessee;

- $417,629 for maintenance and operation of a company park, and an additional $4,032 for volleyball officials, $8,964 for softball officials, and $4,482 for scorekeepers for intracompany games.

Lockheed Martin, a classic welfare mother, can be found in various cities around the country—including the district represented by our number one welfare reformer, Newt Gingrich.

- It's Westinghouse getting to accelerate the depreciation on their machinery (something you and I can't do), saving them $215 million in taxes in 1993 while they eliminated 24,700 jobs.

- It's giving $278 million in government technology subsidies to Amoco, AT&T, Citicorp, Du Pont, General Electric, General Motors, and IBM between 1990 and 1994 while together they cut 339,038 jobs and posted combined profits of $25.2 billion in 1994 alone.

- It's Exxon being able to claim nearly $300 million in tax *deductions* on the settlement they paid when the *Exxon Valdez* spilled 11 million gallons of oil into Prince William Sound.

- It's $11 million to Pillsbury to promote the Pillsbury Dough Boy in foreign countries.

- It's special tax codes that allow Royal Caribbean Cruise Lines to pay *zero* taxes from 1989 to 1992 on a profit of $158 million.

- It's forty-two Fortune 500 companies that paid no federal income taxes from 1981 through 1985 until a minimum tax was forced on them in 1986.

- It's every city in every state in the country forced to clear land, build new roads, upgrade airports, waive local taxes, construct new sewer and water lines, and train thousands of new workers—all at the behest or threat of a corporation that is making record profits and could easily pay for these items themselves.

But why do that when there's welfare? Let us working stiffs pay for the handouts! Why not? We're chumps, and they know it. Hell, we reelected Reagan right in the middle of the biggest looting ever of the American worker—we just said, "Go right ahead and keep sticking it to us!" And they did. And we funded the whole damn raid.

The most audacious moment for these corporate free-loaders came on December 19, 1995, when ninety-one CEOs signed a letter to the President and Congress and ran full-page ads of the letter in newspapers all over the country. In the letter, they demanded that Clinton—get this—*balance the budget*. After more than a decade of Reaganomics, which ran our deficit up to nearly $300 billion, a period when they got wealthy at the expense of millions of us who lost our jobs, they had the gall to demand a balanced budget! Clinton should have gone on TV that night and told them all to go straight to hell. Imagine the wave of cheers across America!

That these CEOs would demand a balanced budget when one of the main reasons the budget isn't balanced is the $170 billion of ADC *they* receive is beyond comprehension.

I think it's time to redefine welfare. Let's stop picking on that nineteen-year-old mother who is trying hard to get by on next to nothing. Doesn't she have enough grief without our moral platitudes? I am happy to pay my $1.14 a day to help the poor. In fact, I'd be willing to double that figure if it meant giving people a cushion till they find their way out of poverty. Hell, triple it!

But when I find out that $1,388 a year of my hard-earned money is going to a bunch of tax-cheating, job-exporting, environment-destroying corporations that are already posting record profits—then I want to track these welfare kings down and tell them it's a new damn day in America. Get off your lazy corporate ass and find new ways to employ Americans, clean up our air and water, and pay your fair share in taxes—or we're going to run your CEO and his cronies off to jail.

To help advance this cause, I would like to present my least favorite corporate welfare mothers—the top CEOs of those corporations who slide their sorry asses up to the federal trough and slop down as much of our tax money as they can. Read carefully the following stories, which detail how these welfare mothers took our money. And keep on the lookout for them, should they come to your town.

WELFARE MOTHER #1

Daniel M. Tellep, Chairman and CEO, Lockheed Martin Corporation

Lockheed Martin, the largest defense contractor in the United States, has been a welfare mother since its inception. Dependent on the government for work in producing weapons and planes, Lockheed was saved from bankruptcy in 1971 by the Nixon administration, thanks to a $250 million federal emergency loan guarantee.

In 1995, Lockheed merged with Martin Marietta and fired up to 30,000 people. The federal government rewarded the top officials of these companies with welfare bonuses of $31 million. While the company denies these payments were related to the merger, the Defense Contract Audit Agency reviewed the payments after considerable media and congressional pressure. They concluded that $4 million of the bonus payment was "unreasonable" and not eligible for federal reimbursement.

In 1989, Martin Marietta decided to throw a free Smokey Robinson concert for its staff and charge $263,000

WELFARE MOTHER #2

**Dwayne O. Andreas, Chairman and CEO,
Archer Daniels Midland**

Archer Daniels Midland calls itself the "supermarket to the world." If the world's supermarket took food stamps, ADM's pocketbook would be overflowing so much that someone would have to call the local welfare cops.

The world price for raw sugar these days is about eleven cents a pound. But the domestic price is double that—twenty-two cents per pound. By paying off politicians over the years, ADM and other sugar interests have successfully lobbied Congress to keep foreign sugar out of this country. This allows ADM to push the corn sweeteners it makes as a "sugar substitute," guaranteeing steady customers and high prices for their product. Profits from the sale of corn sweeteners, along with the production of ethanol, account for nearly half of ADM's yearly profits of over $700 million.

As if this import restriction weren't enough, ADM has persuaded Congress to give it welfare payments of fifty-four cents for every gallon of ethanol it produces, and one dollar for every bushel of corn for the sweetener.

What does this free lunch cost us consumers? According to Tim Wiener, who did much of this research for an article for *The New York Times,* sugar welfare costs us over $3 billion a year more for the sweetened products we buy.

How did this welfare mother get such favorable treatment at the welfare office known as the U.S. Congress? By creating its own welfare system for the politicians. Bob Dole and his foundation have received approximately $470,000 from ADM over the years—his fourth-largest financial backer! They have given him their corporate jet at least twenty-nine times since 1993. ADM has also given Newt Gingrich and his GOPAC organization $70,000 in contributions.

Welfare knows no party, and ADM's payoffs know absolutely no ideological boundaries. The Democrats received $155,000 in 1993 from Andreas, and $100,000 in 1994. He also raised $3.5 million for Bill Clinton's 1992 presidential campaign by throwing a little fund-raising dinner that he cochaired. In 1993, Andreas and his wife were fined eight thousand dollars for exceeding federal limits on political contributions.

This "reverse welfare" has been Andreas's stock-in-trade since the seventies, when he was acquitted of making an illegal $100,000 contribution to Hubert Humphrey's 1968 presidential bid. He also personally brought an envelope stuffed with one thousand $100 bills into the Oval Office and handed it to Richard Nixon in 1972. A check from Andreas for $25,000 was found in the bank account of one of the Watergate burglars.

ADM is currently being investigated by the Justice Department for price-fixing and for its executives' embezzling $9 million, which investigators believe may have been a scheme to move executive income overseas to avoid paying taxes.

Welfare mothers as big as this one will stop at nothing to protect their free ride while the rest of us pay for it.

WELFARE MOTHER #3

Helmut Werner, President, Mercedes-Benz

Nothing upsets us more than foreigners and aliens sneaking into this country and then draining our resources by placing themselves on the public dole. Right?

One such welfare alien is **Mercedes-Benz** of Germany. Unlike most freeloaders who get past our brave border patrol, these Germans actually announced in advance that they were coming. Was the INS waiting for them at customs? Just the opposite! Three different state governments met them with open arms and suitcases full of cash in an attempt to persuade these immigrants to come to their states and deplete their treasuries. North Carolina, South Carolina, and Alabama couldn't wait to put Mercedes on their welfare rolls, and in the end, Alabama won.

So what is Mercedes getting? Two hundred fifty-three million dollars' worth of incentives. The state and federal government will buy the property for them and use the national guard to clear the land. The state will then build roads, enlarge the airport industrial park, develop the factory site, exempt imported components from tariffs, grant tax breaks to suppliers for the plant, provide educational facilities to train managers and teach German families to speak English, purchase 2,500 Mercedes sport vehicles for the state at a cost of $75 million, and rename the freeway between Birmingham and the Mississippi state line the

Mercedes-Benz Highway. All this at a time when the state is facing across-the-board budget cuts.

Maybe I missed the ribbon-cutting ceremony, but that's got to be the first time a state has wanted a road named for a welfare mother.

In return, the Mercedes factory will create 1,500 assembly-line jobs—at a cost to the government of over $170,000 per job!

Perhaps we should show more compassion to these needy foreigners. After all, Mercedes made only $1.51 billion in profits in 1995.

Daimler-Benz, Mercedes's parent company (Germany's largest corporation), has come a long way from the old days when it helped to build Hitler's war machine by using slave labor from the countries he conquered. Maybe our welfare payments to them will make them model citizens.

Alabama *über alles!*

WELFARE MOTHER #4

**Edward A. Brennan, President and CEO,
Sears, Roebuck and Co.**

What happens if you don't do a good job taking care of your money, causing your bank account to nearly run dry? If you're **Sears, Roebuck** you head straight down to the welfare office and sign up for some free *government* cash.

That's what Sears did back in 1989. After running its once-great stores into the ground through poor management and marketing, the company was losing a lot of money. To help balance its ledger, Sears decided to sell its headquarters in Chicago, the Sears Tower, the tallest building in the world. And then it dropped a bombshell—it had decided to move its operations to either Texas or North Carolina. Illinois would lose six thousand jobs. Unless . . .

Unless Illinois made Sears "Welfare Queen for a Day"! And that's exactly what happened. For staying in Illinois (but moving out of Chicago to a suburb called Hoffman Estates), Sears received a $280 million handout. This included $178 million in local tax breaks, plus $61.1 million from the state treasury for site preparation (free streets, sewers, and lights) and $7 million in reduced sales and income tax.

In other words, they got a brand-new headquarters—free of charge, thanks to the taxpayers.

And how did Sears show its appreciation to us for carrying them on our backs? They fired 50,000 people nationwide just four years later—4,900 of them in Illinois! That's the thing about these people on welfare—no fucking gratitude. They take and they take and they take, and right when you're not looking—bam! They wipe you out as if your life means nothing.

Oh, the culture of violence our welfare system has created.

WELFARE MOTHER #5

**Art Modell, Owner/President, the NFL's Baltimore Ravens
(formerly the Cleveland Browns)**

Deadbeat dads are a big problem in our society. They skip town overnight, leaving others to take care of their responsibilities.

The list of National Football League owners who have become wealthy off the fans in one city, only to leave them for greener pastures in another, is getting longer each year. In 1995, Los Angeles lost both the Raiders and the Rams when they moved to Oakland and St. Louis, respectively. By the end of that year, the owner of the Houston Oilers announced his intention to move to Nashville, and Art Modell, President of the Cleveland Browns, told the city he was packing up and moving to Baltimore.

For years, the city of Cleveland had supported Modell and his mediocre Browns with sold-out attendances at nearly every home game played in his drab, ugly, eighty-thousand-seat stadium. The team made a profit. But, as we've learned, there's no such thing as enough profit. So Modell secretly negotiated a deal with Baltimore to move the Browns there.

Baltimore, ironically, had been on the other end of the deadbeat dad syndrome in 1984 when the then-owner of the Baltimore Colts literally had the moving vans pull up in the middle of the night to Memorial Stadium, load up everything the Colts possessed, and truck it off to Indianapolis—new home of the Indianapolis Colts! The city of Baltimore cried foul and protested loudly about how their team had been stolen from them.

I guess they forgot what that felt like as their city leaders stood beaming at the podium with Art Modell, announcing his move from Cleveland to their city. And what kind of welfare did they promise Modell if he came to Baltimore?

How about a brand-new, rent-free stadium built to his personal specifications to the tune of 200 million tax dollars? In addition, Art will get $75 million in "moving expenses," guaranteed season-ticket revenues totaling another $75 million, and millions more in other ticket sales, concessions, parking fees, and advertising. Modell was also given property-tax waivers, 50 percent of the profits from other events (like rock concerts and college games) held in the stadium (plus a 10 percent "management fee"), and rent-free access to, and all revenues from, the old Memorial Stadium while his new stadium is being built.

The city of Cleveland did put up a fight to get their deadbeat dad back, and finally he sent them a little something: they could keep the name "Browns" if they ever got another team going in Cleveland—and they could keep their orange and brown team colors!

It's nice, I think, when a welfare mother or a deadbeat dad gives something back to the community that helped them in their time of need.

Let's Dump on Orange County

A FRIEND OF mine says everything bad in the country comes from California. And he doesn't mean the earthquakes, fires, floods, and riots. His list is long and impressive:

Richard Nixon

Ronald Reagan

John Wayne

All the major defense contractors

Disneyland

The John Birch Society

Congressman Bob Dornan

The anti-immigrant movement
(Prop. 187)

Prop. 13, the anti-tax initiative

The Mighty Ducks

Charles Manson

I told him that, other than Manson, everything he mentioned actually has one connecting thread: *Orange County,* California, a massive sprawl of land and people between Los Angeles and San Diego. Nixon was born there, Reagan got 75 percent of the vote there, and a big statue of the Duke, who lived and died there, greets you upon landing at Orange County's John Wayne Airport.

Orange County has been called the "spiritual base" for America's conservatives—and every loony, right-wing idea we've had to fight over the years seems to have got its start in Orange County. Californians are, naturally, embarrassed by this and often try to shift the blame for our country's rightward drift to Southern rednecks and Bible Belters or, lately, the militias of Montana and Michigan.

But the sad truth is that the Republican Revolution had its birth in groovy California. It's no accident that in 1988 George Bush got more votes per capita in Orange County than in *any other county* in the United States.

Orange County is also one of the wealthiest areas in the country, always ranking up there with the Grosse Pointes and Westchesters and Fairfax Counties as the places that have the greatest concentrations of the well-heeled.

So it came as quite a shock to most people when, on December 6, 1994, Orange County announced it had gone bankrupt. How does one of the richest counties in the country go *bankrupt?* Apparently the county treasurer had, with the approval of the County Board of Supervisors and through the advice of Merrill Lynch, invested huge sums of the taxpayers' money in high-risk "derivatives" that were tied to the fluctuations of the interest rates.

County Treasurer Robert Citron, according to *U.S. News & World Report,* "had borrowed $12.5 billion and poured the money into these derivatives—financial agreements whose values are based on an underlying asset such as a bond. But as the Fed steadily boosted interest rates that year, Orange County got caught in a bind: it had to pay more on its borrowings than it was earning on its investments." This spread led to Orange County's debacle.

Like most of you, I don't have a clue about what I've just quoted, but the rich understand all of this and that's how they got rich in the first place. We would expect the treasurer of Davenport to screw up something this complicated, but not the barons of wealth in Orange County. I think it's embarrassing to have the rest of the world see just how stupid our rich people are.

But that's how it's been for the past fifteen years—lots of dumb rich people taking big risks and making big bucks. Okay, so they aren't *that* stupid. They all got filthy, stinking rich while the rest of the country had to go get a second job to pay the cable bill.

But this high-rolling investment backfired in Orange County—and the residents lost a whopping $1.7 billion of their tax money! The rich, unlike us, get really pissed when they lose that kind of money. (When *we* lose our $30,000-a-year job, we just take more Darvon.)

Blame was thrown everywhere. The treasurer and his assistant were indicted. Merrill Lynch is still being investigated by the SEC. The Orange County Board of Supervisors is claiming ignorance.

The effect of this blowout has been devastating to Orange County. The budget has been cut almost in half. Schools will have to go without renovations or new textbooks. Battered women's shelters have been closed. Prenatal care, police services, and other programs have been cut or eliminated. The California Angels have threatened that they will move if improvements can't be made to the Anaheim stadium. Additions to Disneyland are in jeopardy.

You would think that a group of rich, red-blooded, antitax, antiwelfare conservatives would follow the example of the man who called Orange his home—John Wayne—and just pull themselves up by their own bootstraps.

You would think that these Orange Countiers would take a little personal responsibility for their own actions, maybe even be a little ashamed of losing all that money.

You'd be thinkin' wrong, pardner.

As quick as you can say "free lunch," the leaders of Orange County were running to the state capital in Sacramento and begging for a bailout. They sent a plea to Washington for help. This many rich people had not collectively choked since the *Titanic* hit that iceberg.

The politicians of Sacramento were understandably not all that eager to go out on a limb for the county that has consistently told them to go to hell. How would it look for those politicians to start bailing their constituents' rich butts out of hock when millions of Californians have lost everything they had for far less stupidity?

The legislature told Orange County that charity begins at home and that in the true spirit of volunteerism, they should use their thousand points of light to pass a county-wide tax hike to pay off their own debt.

So they held a tax election in Orange County. Timidly, the county leaders asked their residents to raise their sales tax by just one-half of a penny. That's all—a half-cent! And how did the voters respond? They voted it down, by a three-to-two margin! They felt that *we*—the rest of the country that *they* helped to downsize—should pay for the mess *they* created. Whining and crying like a bunch of babies, they insisted we turn over our hard-earned dollars to them so they can continue living the lifestyle to which they've become accustomed.

And, really, when you think about it, why should they have to give up their Mercedeses, their yachts, and their Performing Arts Center? They worked hard for those luxuries. They pillaged and plundered their way across America, so why shouldn't they have a piece of the cake and eat ours, too?

Without Orange County and its rabid anticommunist movement, we never would have been scared enough of the Evil Soviet Empire to support the defense industry that made Orange County rich in the first place.

Without their backing of Ronald Reagan, the rest of us never would have had the chance to see our real wages decline while their income skyrocketed in Orange County.

If the good people of Orange County hadn't told you to be happy working at your minimum-wage jobs, you wouldn't now be paying the taxes that they want sent to them!

Fortunately, Orange County has come up with a brilliant idea to raise money. They have declared they will open their landfills to their neighbors. Other communities can now bring their trash to Orange County and dump it there—for a fee. The Orange County landfill will accept—at a price of up to $35 a ton—the trash from nearby counties. They are hoping, according to a spokeswoman for the Orange County Integrated Waste Management Department, that they will take in $15 million a year for the next twenty years.

But to do that, they will need to attract five thousand tons of trash a day. That's a lot of garbage, even by California standards, and I worry that they will not be able to meet their quota.

So let's help them out! Send them *your* garbage! It will make you feel good (ah, to dump on Orange County!) and you'll be performing a community service (raising money to help them pay off that $1.7 billion debt). This is reverse Reaganomics in action!

So gather up all your empty Wheaties boxes, your orange(!) juice cans, last night's pizza boxes, those socks with the holes in them, and send them to a private trash hauler contracted to use Orange County's landfill:

Taormina Industries, Inc.
PO Box 309
Anaheim, CA 92815

Taormina has agreed to accept the trash of the people who read this book—provided you send along payment for the dump. In order to comply with U.S. Postal Service regulations, you must make sure that nothing you send has too foul an odor, and that it won't leak, blow up, or emit radiation. It *is* permissible to send garbage. But make sure it is wrapped properly and has the correct amount of postage on it. Mark on the outside PROJECT ORANGE DUMP, and indicate "charitable garbage enclosed." Be sure to enclose payment for the dump. That's $35 a ton, or two cents a pound, plus a couple of extra dollars for handling.

Remember, you are doing this for the good of the country. The people of Orange County have given us so much, and it is only right that we come to them in their hour of need.

A former president now resting in peace in Yorba Linda, Orange County, would be proud.

How to Conduct the Rodney King Commemorative Riot

APRIL 1997 MARKS the fifth anniversary of the L.A. Riots. Since then, many things have happened to improve race relations in Los Angeles. A Republican mayor was elected, a few thousand white people have moved to Arizona, and money raised to rebuild South Central after the riots ended up going toward a construction project in Las Vegas.

CHAPTER 8

Unemployment has risen to 8.6 percent. And, after the O.J. verdict, whites could finally relax and feel okay again about not liking black people. It was just so *awkward* having to do those "black power" handshakes with the "Afro-American" down the hall and trying to remember when to say "Yo!" during the conversation. We white people like the fact that all the "Friends" on TV are white. Like us! It's just more *comfortable* that way.

Ah, Los Angeles. Like the weather, nothing ever changes. If you live in South Central these days, you might as well be living in South Yemen. White L.A. could give two shits about you—and now they aren't even afraid to show it. Five years after Rodney King, the local police have no qualms about beating a truckload of Mexicans with clubs—even if they *know* they are being broadcast live on television!

"Hey, Sarge, look—up in the sky—it's Channel 9!"

"Then get out of the frame [WHACK!] so they can see all this [WHACK!] beautiful blood spewing from this [WHACK! WHACK!] spic's head!"

As the Rodney King anniversary approaches, I'm actually feeling a little sentimental—and I'll bet a lot of black and Hispanic residents in L.A. are, too. Therefore, I've come up with the perfect way for those of you living in South Central to celebrate this special occasion.

Yes, it's time for another riot!

But this time, for the love of God, *don't burn your own neighborhood!* What good does that do? Nothing would make the rest of L.A. happier than to see South Central, Compton, or Watts disappear like so much blow up their rich-ass noses.

I say, if you are upset at The Man, go to where The Man *is*. This time, burn down Beverly Hills! Now, *that* would really send a message. And it would be easy to do.

First, the rich have foolishly built you a *free* road that leads *right to their neighborhoods!* How stupid could they be! This road, called La Cienega (English translation: "The Quagmire"), stretches all the way from Inglewood (just this side of South Central) to Beverly Hills. There are no tolls to pay, no police checkpoints to pass through, no moats, no walls, no identification required. No shoes, no shirt, no service? No problem! Just follow the handy map I've drawn on the next page, and you're on your way.

If you are traveling by car, the trip, during non–rush hours, should take you about twenty to twenty-five minutes.

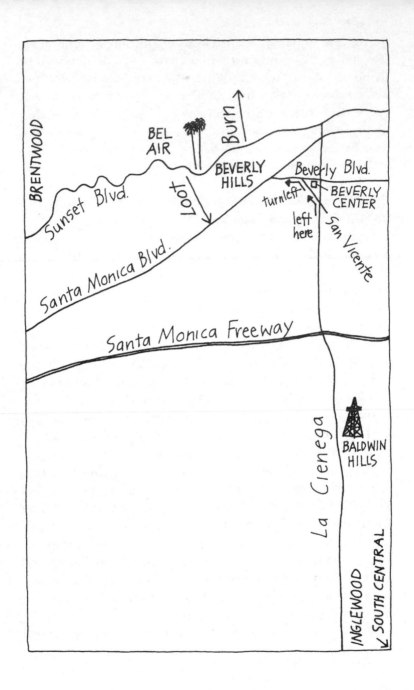

If you are traveling by foot, allow for a little over three hours. Pack a lunch and bring an extra pair of socks for comfort. There are no public facilities along the way, so a portable toilet or a shovel may be in order.

On your way up La Cienega to Beverly Hills, you'll pass the beautiful Baldwin Hills oil field. Again, no security—feel free to stop by if you're a quart low.

Take special note of the newly rebuilt Santa Monica Freeway at the five-mile mark. This overpass, which collapsed in the '94 earthquake, was rebuilt in less than ninety days! Your neighborhood, on the other hand, was destroyed back in **1992** and has yet to see a two-by-four. But don't explode yet, 'cause all the fun is now just two miles away!

As you approach the Beverly Center at the outskirts of Beverly Hills, don't dally with the mall crowd—you've got more important work to do! Take the left fork one block before the mall, onto the street marked "San Vicente." This will take you two blocks to Beverly Boulevard. Turn left and, before you know it, "cee-ment ponds" and Rodeo Drive! Now the excitement can begin.

(*A special note:* Because we *abhor* the loss of human life, please give the residents of Beverly Hills two hours' notice that you're coming. This will give them a head start over the hills and into the safety of the Valley.)

When choosing which facilities to torch, let me suggest those that represent what we like to call our "seats of power." These places, as you know, have kept you on the lowest rungs of the economic ladder for decades. We're talking about anything that resembles a bank (remember the dozen or so times you've been turned down for a loan?), corporate headquarters (know any brothers working *there?*), real estate offices (you mean they've never shown you a home in Costa Mesa?), employment agencies (hey, temp this!), or a liquor store (sure, they're only trying to help you "feel" a little better).

Government buildings are optional, depending on your own personal grievances with the police, the mayor, or the sanitation department. The Metropolitan Transit Authority, which has left South Central off the new subway route and consistently provides you with two-hour waits at the bus stop, is a definite *must*.

I would caution you, though, against taking your aggression out against the entertainment industry. Although this is the number one business in town, well, you see, it's *my* business and I gotta pay the bills! Despite the fact that most blacks have been shut out of Hollywood, I just know the studios mean well, and, hey, I've actually heard them call themselves liberals! Even though most haven't lifted a finger to improve your plight, trust me, they will after this raging inferno.

Most important, I strongly urge you not to view other minorities—Koreans, Vietnamese, Latinos, Jews, Arabs, or Samoans—as your enemy. This is a trick whites have successfully used for the past few hundred years to get you to divert your attention to other groups as the cause of your pain. There is only one "The Man," and I know you know who it is. The Koreans et al., even though they treat you like shit, have just taken their cues from us—proving only that they have fallen for our trick, too.

The issue of looting and burning the homes in Beverly Hills is a judgment call. I would recommend looting the homes between Santa Monica and Sunset (old money, better art to hock) and burning the ones in the hills above Sunset (most of these places are ugly and environmentally unsound, and the higher fires in the hills will allow whites from as far away as Pasadena and Orange County to view the show!).

After you have completed your romp through Beverly Hills, if you still have some gas left in the can, well, you are just a short jaunt from luxurious Bel Air and Brentwood!

Just head west on Sunset, past the hotel where they wouldn't give Eddie Murphy a room in *Beverly Hills Cop*. Beyond that are the neighborhoods where the Reagans and the mayor of Los Angeles live (the Fresh Prince, sadly, has moved).

Finally, after a long and fruitful day of rioting, head back to South Central and get organized. Threaten to visit Malibu next time if you are not given equal access to well-paying jobs, housing, health care, and movies other than just those from the Wayans brothers.

Pagan Babies

WHEN I WAS in Catholic grade school, the nuns would have us adopt what they called "pagan babies." For five dollars a year, I could claim some little child in the Third World as my own. The baby would be baptized with the name I gave him (thus saving the little savage tyke from the eternal desolation of "Limbo"). The five bucks, we were told, would go a long way toward feeding the little innocent, helping him to grow up a strong and loyal Catholic.

CHAPTER 9

One year, when Sister Patricia Marie handed out the baptismal certificates as proof that our pagan babies were now cleansed of Original Sin, there was one extra pagan baby that nobody claimed. So I raised my hand and said it was mine. I figured the more pagans I had under my wing, the better my chances were of escaping the eternal fires of Satan's furnace.

I guess we Americans have always thought of ourselves as a generous people, providing billions in foreign aid to help those in need.

As long as those in need aren't in Gary, Indiana. Or Appalachia. Or Jersey City. Then we turn ruthless—on our *own* people, mind you! We become rabid about cutting all welfare, food stamps, and housing assistance. If you live in Michigan, the governor wants you up and working twelve weeks after you've given birth—or you get no benefits. And he's a Catholic, too!

With so much hatred of our poor here at home, sooner or later, I guess, that sentiment was bound to spill over on the pagan babies overseas. According to the latest polls, most of us—80 percent—think that we're carrying the rest of the world on our shoulders. So it came as a surprise to me to discover that the United States is *last* among the industrialized nations in the amount of foreign aid we distribute per capita.

It turns out that *Saudi Arabia* is the leading humanitarian country in the world, giving more of its GNP to foreign aid—over $5 billion a year!—than any other nation. After Saudi Arabia come Norway, Denmark, Sweden, and the Netherlands. Countries like Portugal and Luxembourg give twice as much as the United States. In total number of dollars, Japan ranks first.

In short, the United States gives less than one half of one percent of our $1.6 trillion budget to foreign aid. But take heart, Americans—we are still number one in providing *military* aid to developing countries.

It was with some interest that I noticed an item in the paper a while back that said conditions in certain parts of the United States had "begun to resemble the Third World." Therefore, the U.S. Agency for International Development (USAID) had decided to provide assistance for the first time *inside* America. USAID was set up to help the poor in developing countries. Now it has put the United States on its list of developing nations! It was an incredible admission on the part of our government that things at home had sunk pretty low. Might we be getting a visit from Sally Struthers sometime soon?

Of course, this wasn't news to many of us who have lived in places like Flint for the past twenty years. Many people who have seen *Roger & Me* have not understood why I included the scene with the woman who raised—and clubbed—rabbits for a living. I wanted people to wonder: "Is this the Third World? Or is it the hometown of the world's richest corporation?!"

This realization—that there are places in the United States that might actually be worse off than the Third World—might be shocking to many, but these days it's all too true.

Take Baltimore, Maryland. Because only 56 percent of the children in Baltimore were immunized, the mayor sought the help of USAID. In 1994 the agency took nine Baltimore health officials to Kenya and Jamaica to see how those countries have accomplished nearly 100 percent immunization. When they got back to Baltimore, they used what they had learned in those Third World nations to get *96 percent* of the kids inoculated against infectious diseases.

USAID has also provided assistance to housing projects in Washington, D.C., and has given consulting services to poverty workers in Boston, Seattle, and other U.S. cities.

This got me thinking. If our own government agrees that the conditions in our inner cities are similar to those in Third World countries, then maybe those cities would also be eligible for foreign aid from the many countries who distribute it. If Canada and Austria and Ireland are giving away millions each year to the Third World, maybe they should be sending some of it to us!

Norway gives the most of the industrialized countries in

percentage of its GNP—over $1 billion. The Netherlands gives over $2 billion.

Would these generous nations be willing to give us a hand, even if our own corporations and government have turned their backs on us? There are so many examples of places here in the United States that could use their help.

I decided to call up many of the governments that are big foreign aid givers.

First up was Norway. The official there, Svein Andreassen, seemed confused by my request.

"It would be very strange if Norway [gave the United States aid]," he told me. "We cannot do anything that would be seen as interfering with the U.S. government. We do have a general sympathy [for these people], as you can see from our printed material."

Next I tried the Japanese, the most generous nation of all in terms of *total* dollars spent. But the embassy guy there said that the request "has to come from your government. We are sending money to many countries. Your country gets other kinds of money from Japan."

The person who answered the phone at the Saudi embassy seemed genuinely interested and asked me to fax my request for aid to "Prince Pandar." Out of respect for Islam, he asked that I leave out any communities that "operate a gambling casino." I said I would, and faxed him the following letter:

Dear Prince Pandar:

Enclosed is my foreign aid request to your government to help out the discarded citizens of my country. Many people here are extremely poor and do not have adequate health care. Thanks to the many generous doctors from the Arab world working in the U.S., we have some hope. But unfortunately our government is very busy balancing a budget and will no

*longer minister to the needs of its own people. I know it
sounds crazy—the richest country in the world and all—but
that's us Americans! A wacky bunch!*

*Thank you for your time. A check in the amount of
$50,000 will go a long way.*

Yours truly,

Michael Moore, American

   If you are a leader of a foreign country and want to send
us some aid, please note the case numbers of the following
neediest cases when sending your check to America.

CASE #156: SHANNON COUNTY, SOUTH DAKOTA

With an unofficial unemployment rate hovering around 80
to 90 percent, Shannon County, South Dakota, home of the
Pine Ridge Indian Reservation, is the poorest county in
America. The average yearly income per person is $3,417—
less than what one would make in Mexico, Argentina, Sin-
gapore, Hong Kong, or South Korea. One in four homes
does not have an indoor toilet. The death rate from alcoholism is nine times the national average. And Congress has
cut housing assistance that goes to Pine Ridge by two-thirds.
   Is there a country out there that can build homes and
help out our native citizens? Send your foreign assistance to:

Oglala Sioux Tribe
PO Box H
Pine Ridge, SD 57770

CASE #71: EL MILAGRO, NEW MEXICO

This village of mostly itinerant Mexican immigrants is one of more than 1,400 such villages that have sprung up in Texas and New Mexico. More than half a million people live here, and fewer than 20 percent are hooked up to a sewer system. One quarter of the people are without running water. Many do not have electricity or telephones. There are places in Bangladesh better off than these neighborhoods. These unsanitary conditions have caused skyrocketing rates of diseases usually found only in the Third World: cholera, dysentery, hepatitis, and dengue fever.

Can you send us a few plumbers from your nation? Contact:

Colonias Development Council
1485 North Main Street
Las Cruces, NM 88001

CASE #922: NATIONWIDE TUBERCULOSIS OUTBREAK

We thought we had eradicated this disease, but it's back and growing steadily in the United States. As of January 1996, about 15 million Americans were infected with TB. There were 26,000 new cases of TB reported in the United States in 1994—compared to 22,930 in Kenya. Before we lose any chance of controlling this epidemic, we desperately need somebody's help.

If you have successfully fought TB in your country, please

tell us how you did it. Send your solution (postcards only) to:

> Centers for Disease Control
> 1600 Clifton Road NE
> Atlanta, GA 30333

CASE #701: NORTHFORK, WEST VIRGINIA

"The medical situation here is basically a Third World condition, like in Ghana," says Christian Anderson—of Ghana—when talking about the Tug River Health Clinic he runs in this rural Appalachian town. Anderson has been unable to get any American doctors to come to Northfork. In fact, Lisa Meredith of the clinic in Northfork told the *Tampa Tribune* that she could not think of one American-born physician practicing in McDowell County. Only doctors from other Third World countries are willing to come here to get the "right training" for their work back home. The best news they've received lately is the donation by Apple of a $2,500 Macintosh computer from the company's Third World Country program.

Can some benevolent country please send us more doctors and money for medicines? Call the Tug River Health Clinic at (304) 862-2588.

CASE #001: WASHINGTON, D.C.

The nation's capital is its own Third World country. In addition to having the country's highest rate of violent crime and the highest number of residents on public assistance, it also has the highest infant mortality rate in the nation. More babies die in D.C., per capita, than in Havana, Cuba.

Public schools couldn't open on time last year because they were deemed "structurally dangerous."

We need a city like Amsterdam to adopt Washington, D.C., as its sister capital and send massive amounts of aid immediately. Hey, you Nethers, are you listening? Put down your bongs and get the hell over here, now! One-way airfare from Amsterdam on KLM to Washington's Dulles Airport is $760 (coach). Once you arrive in southeast D.C., you can pitch in on just about any block.

• • •

I have yet to hear from Prince Pandar, but when I do, I'll pass the check along to West Virginia. In the meantime, review the above cases, and if you are a representative of a nation more generous than the one I belong to, then I beg you to send aid immediately. American readers of this book can send letters to U.S. Agency for International Development, 320 21st Street NW, Washington, D.C. 20523, and ask them to put the above communities on their developing countries list.

Remember, as the good Sisters taught us, the more pagan babies you can save, the better your chances of hanging with the Almighty.

Germany Still Hasn't Paid for Its Sins— and I Intend to Collect

WHERE WAS I during the most exciting part of the fiftieth-anniversary festivities celebrating the end of World War II? You know, when every single German got down on his or her knees, begged for forgiveness, climbed into boxcars in a show of empathy, and then promised to devote one day's salary each week to a Holocaust survivor's family.

Man, that must have been a sight. Did you miss it, too?

A little too harsh, you say, on a country that has already repented and most of whose citizens weren't even alive for all the killing? Hmmm. Let's go to the tote board:

6 million Jews murdered
3 million Catholic Poles murdered
500,000 Gypsies murdered
12,500 homosexuals murdered

Those, plus the Communists, Jehovah's Witnesses, and other undesirables, bring us to a grand total of nearly 10 million defenseless humans slaughtered in the Holocaust. This figure does not include the 400,000 Americans who died in the war (fighting Germany and its partners, the Japanese and Italians), the 25 million Soviet citizens killed or starved to death, plus the millions of other Europeans, Africans, and Asians who died at the hands of what was considered to be the most intelligent, most civilized, most advanced society on earth. And to think, it all happened just a few years ago.

We continue to live with the results of this tragedy. All of our families, Jewish and non-Jewish, were somehow touched by this event. My dad's brother, Lawrence, was killed near Manila. The map of the world is forever screwed up by World War II, and whether it's Bosnia or the Middle East or skinheads terrorizing the residents of Idaho, you can trace the roots of these conflicts back to what the Germans did.

And what was Germany's punishment for these sins? They got to become one of the richest countries in the world! And it took only three decades! How on earth did we let this happen? Today the average German enjoys a standard of living that has no equal. A factory worker in western Germany last year made an average wage of $29 an hour. In the U.S., that same worker made $19. The American worker annually has to put in nearly 200 hours more on the job than his or her German counterpart. That's five 40-hour weeks the Germans don't have to work while they're earning 50 percent more per hour than we Americans. And even though Germany is 25 times smaller in size than the U.S., and has one-third fewer workers, its gross domestic product, per capita, is nearly the *same* as that of the U.S.

Can you imagine, as someone's grandmother was being shoved into the ovens at Auschwitz, an angel appearing to her and saying, "Don't worry, the Germans are going to be rewarded with so much loot, they won't know what to do with it"?

Don't get me wrong. I'm not suggesting that we should have treated Germany the way we did after World War I, humiliating them into submission and starving the country to death. Those conditions certainly created the climate for Hitler to be elected by a majority of the German people. And since the war, many Germans have lived their lives denouncing what their parents did. Young Germans today—if they aren't shaving their heads and beating immigrant domestic workers—are actually very progressive, pacifist, and well-meaning individuals who just happen, through no fault of their own, to be living the good life.

The war may seem like a long time ago, but, according to Daniel Goldhagen, the author of *Hitler's Willing Executioners,* the German government has cataloged more than 330,000 average, everyday Germans who physically participated in the daily slaughter of the Jews. Thousands of those Germans are, *still alive today.* In fact, there are over 12 million Germans still kicking around who were fifteen years or older during World War II.

And what have these Germans done to make some kind of reparation for their sins?

"We don't call it reparation," said the woman on the phone at the German Information Center. "It's restitution."

Okay, so how much "restitution" has Germany decided each life they exterminated is worth? Well, nothing. They won't make any "restitution" for the dead, it was explained to me. But here's the good news! They *will* make up for any *property* loss the Jews suffered. So if you lost a few candlesticks in the Holocaust, step right up for your deutsche marks. Lost your life? Too bad. No *geld* for your loved ones. But . . . if you can prove that you spent "at least six months in a concentration camp," were "confined in a ghetto," or were "forced into hiding for a minimum of eighteen months," then you can collect about $350 to $600 a month from the generous Germans. You say you were only tortured in Dachau for five months and twenty-nine days? Too bad! Sue the Germans and you might get a one-time settlement of $3,000.

To date, Germany has doled out $68.3 billion in "restitution" payments. If we break that down for everyone they killed in the Holocaust, how much is it for each of the 10 million they butchered?

The answer: $6,831.

That's it—$6,831 per mother, father, infant, girl, and boy they gassed, burned, shot, or buried alive. Not a bad price to pay, if it means you can end up one day as the wealthiest nation on earth.

As far as I'm concerned, $6,831 per innocent life is not enough. Not that any amount would be "enough," but my life and your life are worth a little more than $6,831.

I know some of you are saying, "Hey, Mike, the survivors got to move to Israel after the war. Didn't giving them that land make it up to them?" Well, I don't think Israel was actually "given" to them. The British were ruling the place (then called Palestine), and suddenly all these Holocaust survivors with nowhere else to go started arriving and the Brits didn't like that one bit. But they didn't have the energy to fight the Jewish guerrillas after having just lost most of their British empire, so they just bagged the place and said, "Fine, you want this, it's yours." Most Arab residents were not consulted in the deal.

I have never understood why giving the Holocaust survivors Palestine/Israel was such a great gift. Have you ever been there? It's a friggin' desert! There's nothing there! Israelis like to tell you, "We've made the desert bloom!" Talk about rationalizing something . . . I'm telling you, it's 100 percent sand, rock, and more sand. Why did we think we were making it up to them by placing them in a horrible environment that has cost them even more lives in more wars? Because the Bible said so? When did the world start going by *that* book?

If we had really wanted to do what was right—and punish the Germans—we should have given the survivors the state of Bavaria. Now, *that's one* beautiful piece of real estate! And it would have cost the Germans plenty. Turning Palestine into Israel didn't hurt the Germans one single bit. But losing Bavaria to the Jews would have really kicked those krauts where it counted. Israel has only 10,840 square miles; Bavaria has over 70,000! Israel has few, if any, natural resources; Bavaria is rich in minerals, forests, and water. Since the war, the Israelis have been surrounded by hostile enemies who want them dead; Bavaria is surrounded by the beautiful Alps containing a few goats and those three guys in the Ricola commercial. It is probably too late to correct this mistake by moving Tel Aviv to Munich and forcing the Germans to go and try to make the desert bloom.

I'd say that Germany got off real easy. Only 20 percent of its war criminals were ever put on trial. Many who fought in World War II are still alive. And where do you think they all are today?

Florida!

It's true. Tens of thousands of Germans, many of them of World War II age, have permanently moved to the state of Florida. German investment in Florida has increased by nearly 200 percent in the past five years. Together with the British, the Germans provide over 50 percent of the total manufacturing jobs in Florida. They have over $1.8 billion invested in the state. Over on the southwest coast, just in the counties of Collier, Lee, and Charlotte, there are as many as 86,000 Germans.

On a recent trip to southwest Florida, I arrived at the airport in Fort Myers, which has extended its runway so that nonstop jumbo jets to and from Germany can land there. I noticed German flags flying from houses. Everywhere I went there were signs that were printed in German: RAUCHEN VERBOTEN!—NO SMOKING. Menus in restaurants were printed in English *and* German. They are buying up property and businesses and settling in for the good life. And more and more of their friends from the fatherland are joining them.

I am of two minds regarding this German invasion of Florida. On the one hand, I hate Florida. It's full of bugs, humidity, and stupid people running around with guns. And it's got those nutty Cuban exiles. If the President had a big pair of scissors, I wish he'd just snip the state where it hangs off the rest of the country.

But I do like the fact that all these ex-Nazis are moving there to terrorize the people of Florida. Serves them right. The Right-Wing Cubans versus the Geriatric SS in a fight to the finish! I'd pay money to watch that one on Pay-Per-View.

On the other hand, it is ironic that right there in south Florida are thousands of Jewish survivors of the Holocaust. Is it right that those Jewish men and women who fortunately survived the Germans' slaughter should have to be reading menus written in German to accommodate their new "neighbors"? I don't think so.

I have a solution. We all know that Florida is infamous for German tourists being murdered there. I do not believe this phenomenon is the result of gang-related violence. I think it's payback time. One by one, the survivors are getting their revenge. Somebody with a sense of justice has armed the elderly residents of Miami Beach, pointed them in the direction of Fort Myers, and let them loose to even the score. Who would have thought that the Germans would make it this easy for them, foolishly moving to the area that contains the highest concentration of Jews outside of New York? What were these Jerries thinking—that the

Moskowitzes were going to "live and let live," and "turn the other cheek"? Obviously these Germans forgot about the tote board.

I say arm every bingo player south of Fort Lauderdale and let's celebrate the *real* end of World War II. So—RUN FOR YOUR LIFE, KLAUS! And Happy 50th Anniversary!!

So You Want to Kill the President!

I'M AMAZED THAT Clinton hasn't been shot. *U.S. News & World Report* recently felt a need to conduct a poll to find out how many people actually *hate* the President—not disagree with him or dislike him or want to throw him out in the next election. I'm talking about hard-core hatred, the kind that gets you so worked up that tiny lesions begin to develop on your frontal lobes and suddenly you're sitting near a pool of somebody else's blood reading *Catcher in the Rye* for the two hundredth time. That's real hatred. And to think it could all begin by listening to the Rush Limbaugh show!

The Secret Service says that Clinton is the subject of at least 1,500 "very serious" threats on his life each year, and that that number has been rising by

30 percent a year since 1994. Clinton seems destined to set the record as the biggest presidential target ever. On an average of every five hours, Clinton is the recipient of what the Secret Service believes is a "very serious" threat.

Consider what the man has had to put up with:

• Frank Corder steals a Cessna plane, flies to the White House, and crashes it into the wall thirty feet from the President's bedroom.

• Francisco Duran pulls out a semiautomatic rifle on the sidewalk along Pennsylvania Avenue and sprays the White House with twenty-nine bullets while Clinton is watching a football game on TV.

• Leland William Modjeski climbs over the White House fence and gets within fifty feet of the residence before he is tackled by the Secret Service. One of the agents' guns goes off and wounds another agent. Chelsea is inside, having just finished her homework; Mom has already gone to bed; Dad is sneaking a smoke with Leon Panetta.

• Marcelino Corniel, a homeless man, pulls out a knife in front of the White House and is gunned down and killed by the Secret Service.

• An unknown assailant conducts his own drive-by shooting while the Clintons are asleep. Two slugs are found, one in the Clintons' back porch, the other having gone through a window.

The list goes on. There are phone threats from the likes of Gloria Ferrell of Tampa, Florida; stalkers like Ronald Barbour, who followed Clinton while he was jogging; and letter bombs from guys like David Shelby, who wrote: "I hate you . . . Turn Charles Manson loose or I will kill you." He also called for Gore to replace himself with Charles "Tex" Watson, Manson's right-hand man, "or I will kill you in a violent homosexual manner."

Clinton is also the recipient of threats from the Information Superhighway. E-mail messages to the White House have included such statements as "I'm going to blow your little head off," and "I'm curious, Bill, how would you feel about being the first president to be killed on the same day as his wife . . . You will die soon. You can run but you cannot hide." It was signed ALMIGHTY.NEVER.GONNA. CATCH.ME.

What has Clinton done to deserve this? Massacred millions in a war? Caused the stock market to crash? Brought back the bubonic plague? To listen to the Right, you'd think he has brought about the end of Western Civilization—because he smoked a joint? Because he dodged the draft? Because he has an eye for the ladies? For this he deserves to die? C'mon, people! Get a grip!

I suppose these threats on the President's life could be written off as the work of a bunch of kooks. But how would you feel if I told you that these kinds of threats have also come from a United States senator? Or a U.S. congressman? How about a talk-show host? Would that bother you?

It bothers me. And it's happened. And yet, for some strange reason, the Secret Service has not taken any action.

I'm referring to Senator Jesse Helms, Representative Bob Dornan, and talk-show hosts Rush Limbaugh, G. Gordon Liddy, and Oliver North. They have each offered some sort of veiled or obvious threat that, in essence, has said that Clinton had better watch it or harm will come to him.

The most vicious of these came on November 22, 1994 (the 31st anniversary of Kennedy's assassination). Senator Jesse Helms of North Carolina issued the following threat to the President: "Mr. Clinton better watch out if he comes down here [to North Carolina]. He'd better have a bodyguard." This comment came two days after the right-wing Helms implied that military men hated Clinton, their commander-in-chief, adding, "We got a pile of military installations in North Carolina." He said military men were upset over Clinton's draft dodging, his support of gays in the military, and his desire to cut the Pentagon's budget.

On January 26, 1995, Representative Bob Dornan of Orange County, California, went on PBS, telling Judy Woodruff, "I can't wait till we're rid of this shallow human being . . . most military people agree with me. . . . He was a leader in the pro-Hanoi movement."

Or how about this gem from Rush Limbaugh, who instructed his listeners: "The second violent American Revolution is just about—I got my fingers about a quarter of an inch apart—is about that far away . . . because these people are sick and tired of a bunch of bureaucrats." (One of Limbaugh's "dittohead" fans who threatened to kill the President spoke from his jail cell about loving Rush's "polemics" on Clinton.)

G. Gordon Liddy bragged about how he drew stick figures on targets and named them Bill and Hillary because he thought it would improve his aim when he practiced firing his guns. He told a caller that when the feds come to your door to "kill your wife and children . . . use that Garand [M-1 rifle], and it'll take 'em out."

CALLER: "And yes, aim for the head . . . I'm aiming between the eyes."

LIDDY: "Absolutely . . . That way their flak jackets won't protect them."

What I have wondered for the better part of the past two years is why none of these individuals were arrested for threatening the life of the President. The federal law on this is very clear:

> *Whoever knowingly or willfully . . . deliver[s] . . . any threat to take the life of or to inflict bodily harm upon the President of the United States [or] makes any such threat against the President . . . shall be fined not more than*

$1,000 or imprisoned not more than five years, or both.
[18 USC Section 871]

When Senator Jesse Helms warns the President that he'll need a bodyguard if he comes to his state, that sounds like a threat to me.

Numerous cases have clarified exactly what the law means by a "threat," and from my reading of it, there is enough evidence to support the prosecution of Jesse Helms.

In *United States v. Patillo,* the court ruled that a threat constitutes statements that are intended "to incite others to injure him or restrict [the President's] movements"—like visiting North Carolina. In *Roy v. United States,* the court ruled that "even if the threat was a joke, the defendant was properly found guilty of knowingly and willfully threatening the life of the President" because the threat was made "from a Marine base where Marines were stationed with access to weapons and ammunition. The President was due to arrive [on the base] . . ." Note the references Helms made regarding all the military bases in North Carolina and the anger that military men have toward Clinton.

The law says you don't even need intent to carry out the threat—just *implying* the threat is enough for prosecution. One ruling, dating from 1918, stated the following: "A statement by the accused, after applying vile epithets to President Wilson, that he wished the President was in hell, and that if he had the power he would put him there, was a threat against the President in violation of [the law]."

So even though Helms later said his threat was a "mistake," like most crimes, after you commit them you can say you're sorry all you want, but you're still going to court.

Senator Helms made a definite threat against the President of the United States. The others (Liddy et al.) made clear calls for violence, and used violent language calling for someone to "get rid" of Clinton and announcing that a "violent revolution" was at hand.

So why haven't Helms and company been prosecuted? In the late seventies, some crazy guy in Flint got on a city bus and started screaming that he was going to kill Jimmy Carter. He was arrested, tried, and sentenced to federal prison. Is Helms getting special treatment because he is a United States senator?

My researcher Tia Lessin decided to call up the Secret Service in Washington to find out why Helms avoided prosecution. She reached an agent on the duty desk who agreed to talk to her without using his name. What he told her was quite surprising.

I want to make a formal complaint regarding a threat made by Senator Helms against the President.
> Once we saw that on the news and we heard it, we did a complete investigation.

You did a complete investigation?
> Yeah.

And what charges have been issued against the Senator?
> No charges have been issued. He came out afterwards and apologized and said he didn't mean that—that he didn't mean to be threatening and that type of thing.

But according to the U.S. Code, whoever knowingly and willfully makes any threat to take the life of the President, or afflicts bodily harm upon the President, "shall be fined not more than one thousand dollars or imprisoned not more than five years or both." Was the Senator fined?
> No, he wasn't. . . . We presented this [investigation] to the U.S. Attorney's office and they chose, for whatever reasons, they chose not to prosecute. Ultimately that is going to be their decision.

Did the Secret Service make a recommendation to prosecute?
Yes.

Oh, you did?
Yes, we always do on these cases. We take it very seriously.

So you were concerned enough to make a recommendation to prosecute the Senator, but the U.S. Attorney's office found against that?
That is correct.

They are kind of undercutting you guys by not prosecuting people like that.
Well, generally they do. Usually the rule of thumb they take is whether the person was serious when they made the threat. . . . If the person is drunk and at a bar, once they sober up, we generally don't prosecute those people.

Was the Senator drunk at the time?
Probably not.

He basically offered up to the military this proposition: "Why don't you take him out?"
I agree with you, I think it was highly inappropriate.

It was inappropriate and irresponsible and seems like it was also against the law.
You're absolutely right.

He broke the law.
That's correct. . . . He clearly stepped over the line. I think if it happens again, if it is repeated, you will see him prosecuted.

I know you guys keep a database of a list of folks who made threats against the President, and they never come off that list?
That's correct.

Is Helms on that list now?
Sure.

So he's part of your database? You're keeping an eye out for him?
Anybody we interview or anybody who makes some kind of comment, we interview them and we keep the information stored here.

You interviewed Mr. Helms?
Uh-huh. He was interviewed.

Oh, really? Once? Twice?
To tell you the truth, I have not read the case recently, but I'm sure it was just once.

Well, that makes me feel better, knowing that there is a file on Jesse Helms and to some degree you guys are following him.
Absolutely.

I mean, are you looking at his congressional statements on the Senate floor?
You bet.

You're following what he says in North Carolina and other places?
Sure. We do have a couple of agents assigned to the Capitol, and we have a couple of analysts who watch all of the papers and the media and all those type of things.

Did [your] morale kind of go down when the U.S. attorney's office decided not to follow up on your recommendation?

To tell you the truth, I don't think it surprised anybody. We didn't expect him to go to jail for that. Although we disagreed with it strongly, I didn't really expect him to go to jail over it.

I would like to make an example out of this guy Helms, 'cause he's certainly made an example out of himself. It seems like you would be sending a message out to folks if you prosecuted him.

I agree with you. But again, it was a very political decision.

Let me ask you this: If Senator Helms makes another threat, I think we all should be on guard and listen to him closely, not just leave it to you guys, because you're overburdened. If we all took it upon ourselves to monitor the Helmses and the Liddys, and if we heard something that went past you guys, how would we report that to you?

I would recommend just contacting the local office. We have field offices in most major U.S. cities.

Thank you. We will do that.

• • •

There it is, readers. The challenge is ours. If you hear Helms or others make a threat against the President, call your local Secret Service office and file a complaint (see the following list of Secret Service numbers). They will take these complaints seriously and have promised to take action.

Maybe the next time Senator Helms shoots his mouth off, he'll end up spending a few years fighting Hinckley for the top bunk.

YOUR LOCAL SECRET SERVICE AGENTS

Atlanta: Raymond A. Shaddick (404) 331-6111
Austin: Ms. Shawn M. Campbell (512) 916-5103
Baltimore: Richard A. Rohde (410) 962-2200
Bismarck: Richard K. Oliver (701) 255-3294
Boise: Dennis L. Morgan (208) 334-1403
Boston: Richard A. Elkowitz (617) 565-5640
Buffalo: Howard I. Hendershot (716) 551-4401
Charlotte: Kevin Foley (704) 523-9583
Chicago: Ralph L. Grayson (312) 353-5431
Cincinnati: Richard K. Rathmell Jr. (513) 684-3585
Cleveland: Michael S. Young (216) 522-4365
Dallas: Jerry P. Patton (214) 868-3200
Dayton: Larry J. Larrimer (513) 222-2013
Denver: Edward Zahren (303) 866-1010
Des Moines: Jerry J. Weber (515) 284-4565
Detroit: Richard L. Hartman (313) 226-6400
Houston: James P. Dale (713) 868-2299
Indianapolis: Dennis Kinley (317) 226-6444
Jacksonville: Rafael A. Calzada (904) 232-2777
Kansas City: Douglas W. Buchholz (816) 374-6102
Las Vegas: Joseph J. Saitta (702) 388-6446
Little Rock: Bill Aicher (501) 324-6241
Los Angeles: James E. Bauer (213) 894-4830
Louisville: Karen T. Barry (502) 582-5171
Madison: Robert A. Timmel (608) 264-5191
Miami: Jack E. Kippenberger (305) 591-3660
Milwaukee: Robert F. Byers (414) 297-3587

Minneapolis: Thomas A. Pabst (612) 348-1800
Nashville: Thomas J. Caul (615) 736-5841
New Haven: Robert J. Kasdon (203) 868-2449
New Orleans: Dennis R. Satterlee (504) 589-4041
New York: Brian F. Gimlett (212) 637-4500
Oklahoma City: Joseph L. Gallo (405) 297-5020
Orlando: Eric S. Johnson (407) 648-6333
Philadelphia: Ernest J. Kun (215) 597-0600
Phoenix: James R. Lukash (602) 640-5580
Pittsburgh: Daniel E. Mayer (412) 644-3384
Portland: Marc Tinsley (503) 326-2162
Raleigh: Patrick C. Smith (919) 790-2834
Sacramento: Louis T. Alexander (916) 498-5141
Saginaw: Lawrence R. Porte (517) 752-8076
St. Louis: Donald M. Schneider (314) 539-2238
San Diego: Joseph J. Perez Jr. (619) 557-5640
San Francisco: Leroy G. DalPorto (415) 744-9026
Seattle: Charles Brewster (206) 220-6800
Toledo: Gary A. Bianchi (419) 259-6434
Wilmington: Joseph M. Casper (910) 343-4411

Show Trials I'd Like to See

THE ONE THING I always liked about the Red Chinese was their show trials. They grabbed a guy who they thought did something offensive against the state and then put him on trial in a big arena so everyone could show up and denounce the traitor. Even though there were "prosecutors" and "defenders" and "judges," it was all just a show, 'cause the fix was already in. The guy was going to hang, no matter what.

But it was great entertainment and it made everybody feel good about the Revolution, a sort of mass catharsis to take it all out on one miserable soul who probably deserved it in the first place. As we know in our own country, if the police arrested him, he must have done *something* wrong.

For some strange reason, I've been

CHAPTER 12

having a lot of dreams about this lately. Show Trial dreams. Every night a new defendant is in the dock. The trials all take place sometime in the future. The forces of good have won out and we are now in charge—the disgruntled postal workers, the overworked MCI operators, the seven-year-olds whose parents insist that they fly their own planes. They now call the shots.

Each night, in these dreams, the accused stands on the fifty-yard line in Giants Stadium. Eighty thousand rabid citizens have packed the place to demand justice. A tribunal of judges sits on a raised platform in the end zone. The judges are Ed Asner, John F. Kennedy Jr., and MTV's Daisy Fuentes (don't ask me why). The prosecutor is Marlon Brando and the defense attorney is John Tesh (yes, he was allowed to live after the revolution). The defendant, upon learning that John Tesh is the one responsible for saving his life, always asks the judges if he can defend himself.

Here, to the best of my recollection, is how some of the dreams have been going.

Show Trial Dream #1
"The People v. *Saturday Night Live*"

All writers and performers for the past sixteen years are forced to watch every show since 1980. Then they are forced to watch them again. Those without a good explanation for these shows are "taken away." (Mike Myers, Dana Carvey, and Eddie Murphy are found "not guilty.")

Show Trial Dream #2
"The People v. the NRA"

After the guilty verdict, the board of directors of the National Rifle Association are given a five-second head start. A gang of disenchanted youths whips out its automatic weapons and chases the NRAers across the field with a spray of bullets.

Show Trial Dream #3
"The People v. Henry Kissinger"

In this dream, Kissinger is asked to explain the secret bombing of Cambodia, but before he finishes, the judges just go ahead and find him guilty of war crimes. He is stripped naked and told to get on all fours and bark like a dog. Then Vietnamese amputees encircle the former Secretary of State and beat him silly. All the while, Joan Baez gets the crowd to join her in a version of "O Happy Day!"

Show Trial Dream #4
"The People v. the Guy Responsible for the Little Silver Tape You Can't Get Off the CD Box"

The inventor of this annoying, impossible, never-get-the-sticky-stuff-off-the-box little piece of silver tape is just taken to the fifty-yard line and shot.

Show Trial Dream #5
"The People v. Senator Strom Thurmond"

Senator Thurmond, during this trial, refuses to recognize the jurisdiction of the court and has to be bound and gagged for the proceedings. He is then forced to watch two men enjoy a long, deep kiss. (The dream then skipped ahead to a doctor telling Thurmond's next of kin something about an "aneurysm.")

If Clinton Had Balls . . .

CHAPTER 13

BILL CLINTON WAS the first major party candidate I had voted for in a long time. To be precise, *I* didn't actually vote for him. My daughter, Natalie, who was eleven at the time, wanted to see the voting booth, so I let her come in and pull the lever. Later I found out that it's illegal to let a child vote, but, hey, I didn't want any blood on *my* hands, voting for Clinton. I just felt, you know, so . . . *uneasy* about the guy. He reminded me of that wonk who ran for senior class president and was so ambitious about *winning* that he'd say or do anything to get elected.

Earlier, when Clinton was campaigning in Flint, I went to listen to him speak. As I stood in the back of the union hall, one of his aides spotted me, whispered something to Clinton, and then came over to where I was standing.

He said that Governor Clinton had seen *Roger & Me* and had been quite moved by it and would like to meet me. You know, just a little photo op for the hometown cameras. No thanks, I said. Oh, and by the way, what's he doing here in a union hall when he plans to ship these folks' jobs to Mexico?

But by election night back in 1992, I felt that the Dark Ages of Reagan and Bush had to come to an end. So little Natalie—who justified her action by saying she was "really doing it for Hillary"—voted in her first election, and Clinton became our 42d President.

To put it mildly, I couldn't believe Clinton's first five days in office. It felt as though we had just spent twelve years crossing the Republican desert and had finally arrived in the Promised Land. During his first week in office, Clinton signed a number of executive orders and policy directives that wasted no time in showing this country that, when it came to dealing with the right wing, this guy had ridden into town with his shitkicking boots on. With a stroke of the pen he:

- Lifted the ban on federally funded health care clinics discussing abortion;

- Lifted the ban on abortions being performed on overseas military bases;

- Ordered the birth control drug RU-486 to be prepared for availability in the U.S.;

- Lifted the ban on medical research on fetal tissue;

- Ordered international aid to be reinstated to foreign countries whose health agencies perform abortions.

I couldn't believe it. If Clinton hadn't inhaled, I must have. The Right to Lifers were going insane, and I couldn't have been happier. His first week in office was a stunner.

But before the hangover from the party I was throwing in

my head had worn off, ol' Bill was doing a backpedal the likes of which hadn't been seen since Jimmy Swaggart tried to explain why he had written a bad check to a prostitute.

Clinton began his Olympic-style flip-flops by backing down on gays in the military. After months of talking about lifting the ban, he came up with his goofy Don't Ask, Don't Tell policy. Then he backed down on his comprehensive health care plan, which he had promised to enact within his first hundred days in office. By the end of those hundred days, he was the only one who had the free doctor. One year later, he held up a pen during his State of the Union message and said, "This is the pen I will use to veto any health care bill that does not have one hundred percent universal coverage for all Americans." Six months later he reduced that number to 95 percent. By the end of the year, he was saying everything was open to compromise.

Or maybe he just misplaced that pen. Maybe Bob Dole swiped it from him and is still holding it. I don't know. By 1994 the congressional Democrats declared that health care reform was dead.

The list of flip-flops became embarrassing. He nominated Lani Guinier as assistant attorney general for civil rights, and then, as soon as the Republicans said, "Boo!" he withdrew her nomination, saying he "hadn't read" some things she had written.

He offered this same kind of courageous nonsupport for his Surgeon General, Joycelyn Elders, when she said boys and girls should be taught about masturbation. She also said we should consider legalizing drugs. Oops. Sex, drugs, and she was rock-and-rolled back to Arkansas. He'd thrown the Republicans another bone.

But they just wanted more blood—and they got it with Dr. Henry Foster, Clinton's nominee to replace Elders. As quick as you can say "first trimester," Foster was gone. His crime? He had performed *legal* abortions. Instead of telling the Right to Lifers where to go, Clinton shuffled his feet, bowed his head, and did one more retreat.

Clinton's reversals weren't limited to domestic policy. During the campaign, he charged that Bush's policy of returning Haitian refugees to Haiti was "illegal." But no sooner had he heard "Hail to the Chief" played for the first time than he began ordering the Coast Guard to kick every Haitian ass they found at sea back to Haiti.

Clinton had also chided Bush for "coddling up to" the regime in Beijing, placing U.S. business interests in China over human rights. So when Bill got to sit in the big chair in the Oval Office, what did he do about China? What any self-respecting redneck does when he's got new wheels—spin around and do a 180! "Yeeeeeehhaaaawwwwwww! China, here we come—let's trade!"

George Bush must have been puking up those pork rinds.

Remember "Peacenik Bill"? I admired how, during the campaign, he stood up to all those flag-waving morons and, in essence, admitted, "Yeah, that's right, I wasn't going to Vietnam, no way, no how—and I was going to kiss the ass of every ROTC commandant I could find to make sure I would never kill any Vietnamese." Throughout the campaign, he never backed down from that basic position. You had to be smart to beat Uncle Sam at his own game back in the sixties, especially when the good uncle wanted to offer you up as a sacrifice on the altar of false patriotism. Clinton's little scam was his version of "Alice's Restaurant." I figured he deserved to be president.

But, damn, within just two years after this ex-sort-of-hippie is elected, he orders a $25 billion increase in the budget for the Pentagon, including an additional B-2 bomber that his own Defense Secretary told him was a waste of money. Where have all the flowers gone, Bill?

You would think that when the Republicans took over Congress in 1995 with their Contract *on* America, Clinton would have been ready to do battle. Wrong! He found that damn pen he had lost for the health care bill and quickly signed the first two Contract provisions passed by the Republican Congress. He then pledged to look favorably at the other bills they would send to him.

There was a brief moment when I thought Clinton had discovered why we sent him to Washington. Immediately after the Oklahoma City bombing, he lashed out at the hatred that Republicans had been fueling around the country and had the courage to link this climate of hate to the bombing. He stood up to the NRA, the right-wing talk-show lunatics, and all the others who had been pushing this loathing of the federal government. Now 168 federal employees and their children were dead, and Clinton wasn't pulling any punches. It was great to see him fighting—and what was the result? THE RIGHT WING BACKED DOWN! They were on the defensive, on the run, and the rest of the year was a miserable one for them. The Contract with America bills came to a virtual halt, and their efforts to close down the federal government so many times became their Waterloo.

You would think Clinton would have learned something from this. But as the 1996 election neared, he began sounding more and more like a Republican. His State of the Union Address was lauded for stealing the Republicans' thunder when he announced that "the era of big government is over." (Hey, buddy, you only exist *because* of "big government." From your mother's job in the county hospital to your college grants to every single job you've had since you became an adult, you are a total product of the kindness that comes from "big government.")

Where are this man's balls? He has embarrassed himself and those of us who voted for him. Most people in this country find it hard to respect him. You want to like the guy—at his core, he comes from the same working-class place most of us are from. When he's his honest, Big Mac–eating, sax-playing, hillbilly self, we like the guy. But some little voice in his head apparently keeps whispering, "Moderate, Bill, moderate, and the people will love you."

Bill, if you're reading this, hire an exorcist and kill that demon inside you! The truth is this: the American people today do not want moderation, they want aggressive action. According to a study of the 1994 election, conducted by Leonard Williams and Neil Wollman of Indiana's Manchester College, Democratic incumbents (like you) who tried to take a more conservative position *lost the election!* Those who stuck to their *liberal* ideals actually *won*—especially in districts that were considered vulnerable for Democrats. The study concluded:

> *Being a liberal, as opposed to a moderate Democrat, actually enhanced significantly one's likelihood of election success.*

In other words, the public these days *hates* the middle of the road, and doesn't trust anyone who travels there.

Bill, you have been misled into thinking that, by appealing to the middle-of-the-road conservative white man, you will get reelected. You couldn't be more wrong. Forget those guys! They have a party, it's called Republican, and nothing you say or do will persuade them to love you. Do you realize that no Democratic president since Roosevelt, other than Lyndon Johnson, has received the majority of the white male vote? Not Truman, not Kennedy, not Carter, not even you. They and you all won by getting the overwhelming majority of women and minorities, plus a *minority* of white men, out to the polls on election day. So focus all your efforts on addressing the needs of women, blacks, Hispanics, and the white guys like me, and you'll be given one more chance to do some good for the country in the next four years.

Bill, if you had had the courage of your convictions and could have gotten it through your thick head that you actually *won* in 1992, you would have spent the past four years giving your opponents this very simple message:

> *I am right, and you are wrong. This is the way it is going to be done. I will bark, and you will jump. And you will ask, "H.. .w high, Mr. President?" You will like it or lump it— a.id if you lump it, you can throw me out of office in four years. But until then, the people have spoken, and they have said that they are fed up with the policies of the Reagan and Bush administrations. So fuck off and good night!*

We have never heard that speech, have we? Reagan gave a version of it when he took office. Hinckley shot him a month or so later. Reagan came out of the hospital even more pissed, and we paid for it through the eighties. Clinton never had Reagan's balls, so our side never had a chance.

What a shame. What a waste. What a wuss.

Steve Forbes Was an Alien

WHERE DID STEVE FORBES come from? And where has he gone?

I had never heard of the guy until 1996. I had heard of his magazine, *Forbes,* a magazine for rich people. I had even met the man they said was his father, Malcolm Forbes Sr. He had motorcycled to the *Roger & Me* premiere in New York and proceeded to come inside and taunt me. But who was "Steve"?

CHAPTER 14

In the early '96 primaries, Steve Forbes spent $30 million of his own money to buy his way onto the ballot and into the public's consciousness. But there was something about him, something beyond the usual politician weirdness that I couldn't figure out, something that seemed so . . . odd.

Then one night I saw Steve Forbes on "Nightline." Ted Koppel asked him a question and, I swear, Forbes went an entire minute and a half AND NEVER ONCE BLINKED HIS EYES!

Thinking this was highly unusual, I called Mount Sinai Hospital and asked for the opthalmology unit. I asked the intern who picked up the phone just how often our eyes need to blink. He told me that humans have to blink their eyes at least once every fifteen seconds. I confirmed this with an optometrist, Dr. Stuart Blankman, at his office in New York. He said that the average person blinks his or her eyes between twelve and fifteen times per minute, although one could go as long as twenty seconds. "I doubt if anyone would only blink once in thirty seconds."

I called the doctor back at Mount Sinai, and he said that to go for a full minute would cause involuntary tears. I told him this guy Forbes went an entire minute and a half—and his lids didn't budge!

"That's not possible," the doctor assured me. "*You* must have blinked when Forbes blinked, and that's why you missed it. To go that long without blinking? That's not humanly possible."

Not . . . human?

The next night, Forbes was on CNN, and there he was, doing it again—NOT BLINKING! I called my wife, Kathleen, into the room.

"Now watch closely. Do you see him blinking? He's not blinking, is he?"

"No, he's not blinking," she said, hoping I would be satisfied so she could go back to more important matters.

"No, he's not," I replied. *"And he won't. Not now, not ever! He's not human!"*

"Well, then, for God's sake," she screamed in mock horror, *"don't look into his eyes!"*

I immediately averted my eyes, listening only to the sound of his Yankee whine as he repeated, over and over— as if to put us in a trance—the words "flat tax . . . flat tax . . .

flat tax . . . flat tax . . . flat tax . . . flat tax . . . flat tax . . . flat tax . . ."

I turned off the TV—but it was too late. The entire nation had begun the same precise chant: "Flat tax . . . flat tax . . ." The polls in New Hampshire showed him overtaking Senator Dole. How was this happening? Then I figured it out. All the pod people live in New Hampshire!

Was I the only one who had figured it out? I became convinced that future civilizations must know the truth about what happened to us.

From my diary, 2/4/96:

> *Shortly before the millennium's end, millions on our planet began to disappear. At first they called it "downsizing." We thought the rich were behind this. We didn't realize these men known as "CEOs" were actually invaders from another planet. We should have figured it out. They all read a magazine with their leader's name on the cover. Forbes. We should have seen it coming. Before long, everyone had been "downsized"—and now I am among the few left to record what has happened to our civilization. . . .*

The following week, I was in Des Moines, Iowa, four days before the Iowa caucuses. I decided to get up the courage and visit Forbes's headquarters and confront him with the truth. Steve Forbes was not there when I arrived, but a campaign coordinator agreed to step outside and talk to me.

"Who are you?" I asked.

"My name is . . . Chip Carter," he responded.

Chip Carter! My God, they've taken the former president's son! I tried to keep my composure and not let on that I knew he was not who he said he was.

"Can you tell me where Steve Forbes is from?" I asked, knowing that to give me an honest answer would possibly violate Starfleet's orders.

"Somewhere out there," he said—pointing upward to the sky! (I swear this happened exactly as I'm telling it to you now. To confirm it, contact the students at the TV station at Iowa State in Ames, Iowa. They were there and witnessed this entire exchange.)

I continued with "Chip."

"How long has he . . . been here?" I asked nervously.

"He has been on the ground twenty-eight days," Chip said.

On the ground!

"Where will he go next?"

"Oklahoma."

Oklahoma! My God!

"And where will you travel to?"

"I am awaiting orders from Headquarters."

At that point, he abruptly ended the conversation, perhaps knowing that he had released too much information to a civilian/specimen. Could he tell just by looking at me that I had yet to be "downsized"? That night, at the Des Moines Ramada Inn, I was a wreck.

A few weeks later, Steve Forbes was suddenly gone. Were the forces of good too much for this "man"? Forbes did win Delaware and Arizona—two states I can guarantee you I will NOT be visiting anytime soon. After a brief appearance on a comatose late-night Saturday show, where I swear I saw him wearing a longhaired wig and an Aerosmith T-shirt (an obvious ploy to get to our young and steal their brain matter), he was gone.

Will this strange man ever return? I do not know. His magazine, though, is still with us. Eternal vigilance may be our only hope. Beware the body snatchers who promise you the flat tax!

Parents, you've been warned.

Corporate Crooks Trading Cards

LET'S PLAY WORD association. I say a word, you tell me the first thing that pops into your head. Ready?

Crime.

"Murder!" "Robbery!" "Car theft!"

Criminal.

"Big black guy!" "Mountain man building bombs in a 10 × 12 shack!"

Outstanding. You've correctly identified the popular images associated with crime and criminals. And the

CHAPTER 15

FBI agrees with you. Each year they release a bunch of crime statistics that all refer to criminals who mug us, break into our homes, or assault us.

The issue of crime is always at the top of the political agenda. Voters list it as one of their primary concerns. Politicians exploit it by railing against the criminal element and offering new bills in Congress guaranteed to make our streets safer by locking up all the bad guys and throwing the key away.

We have become a frightened nation, triple deadbolting our doors, fastening The Club to our parked cars, always on guard for what may lurk around the next dark corner.

But what would you say if I told you that there is a far greater threat out there, one so sinister that it causes much more harm and havoc than any gang of Crips or Bloods? And to make matters worse, what if there is a criminal element out there that doesn't look anything like thugs, but rather acts as if they are your friends. People you can trust. People we actually reward even after they've ripped us off or caused the death of a loved one.

What if I told you that Corporate Crime—or its media-friendly term, "White Collar Crime"—causes *more deaths* and costs you *more money* each year than all the street criminals combined? Seems impossible, doesn't it? But it's true. In 1994, burglaries and robberies cost us over $4 billion in losses, while corporate fraud cost us nearly $200 billion! Or how about this statistic: handguns last year caused around 15,000 deaths. Unsafe working conditions on the job and occupational diseases caused more than 56,000 deaths.

Why aren't we as appalled by this as we are when some punk pulls out a gun and shoots a clerk behind the counter? Why is it that when the *company* that employs the clerk knowingly has faulty wiring in the basement, resulting in a fire that kills the clerk, we don't feel the same outrage? Or why is it that when some junkie breaks into our home and steals our stereo we want to strangle the bastard, but when the company that makes that stereo conspires with other companies to prevent the cost of CDs from ever going down—thus ripping us off of hundreds of dollars—we don't call for the same swift justice?

We've been persuaded to see "criminals" as our true

threat—and it works. It works especially well for the white middle class because the crooks are often not of our economic class or skin color. They are the perfect fall guys for all our frustration.

We've been convinced that corporate executives are like gods, that they keep the country rolling along, and—here's the best part—if we work hard enough, we can grow up to be just like them!

I think it's time to redefine crime. When the individuals running a savings and loan loot the life savings of an elderly couple, that should be a crime. When corporate executives approve the dumping of pollution into the air or water, causing untold environmental damage and eventually killing thousands of people, that should be a crime. When a CEO defrauds the federal government on a defense contract, stealing our tax money, that, too, should be a crime. And when an automaker decides to save eleven dollars on a safety part, the omission of which causes the deaths of dozens of people, that should definitely be considered a major crime.

These corporate crimes should be listed as serious felonies, even more serious than the crimes committed by street criminals. Why? Because, unlike many of the street criminals who violate the law because they're high on PCP or are so mentally gone they can't find an honest way out of their predicament, the corporate criminal knows *exactly* what he is doing and why he is doing it. His motive is pure greed.

The man in the three-piece suit is ripping us off not because he needs to put food on his table or a roof over his head. He's stealing from us because the wealth he has already accumulated *just isn't enough!* He wants a house in the South of France. He wants to invest in another South African diamond mine. His competition has a bigger yacht and it's driving him crazy.

To me, that person is a thousand times more criminal and *immoral* than the crazy son of a bitch who stole my color TV.

(In the interests of full disclosure, just so you don't think I have a special place in my heart for street criminals, I've been the proud victim in my life of seven B&Es, an arson at the place where I worked, a broken arm caused by a drunk driver who ran into me, a guy with a knife coming after me, another guy waving a gun in my face, and a mugger sticking me up in Times Square when I was fourteen and taking all of thirty-seven cents from me at knifepoint. So I hate these fuckers and I strongly believe in removing all dangerous people and putting them somewhere that I'm not.)

We have all had similar experiences. But can we be smart enough and courageous enough to start looking at "crime" in a different way?

On "TV Nation" we created Crackers, the Corporate Crime Fighting Chicken, as the show's mascot. We figured street crime fighters already had McGruff, the Crime Fighting Dog—but who was out there fighting *corporate* crime? So we sent Crackers on a tour of the country. The response was phenomenal. Wherever he showed up to ask citizens to report the corporate criminals in their area, thousands of people would descend on his Corporate Crimemobile. So many people showed up, desperate to see Crackers, when he arrived in Daley Plaza in Chicago that the Chicago police shut us down. Crackers's 800 number received more than 30,000 corporate crime tips. It was the most amazing thing I had ever seen. It was clear to me that America was indeed ready to take on the corporate crooks who had made our lives, our homes, and our workplaces less safe.

In order to continue our corporate-crime-fighting ways, I've decided we need something to remind us who the dangerous corporate criminals are, something that we can use to warn others of their evil ways. I would like to introduce to you the brand-new Michael Moore Corporate Crooks Trading Cards. Each card is listed below, with a handsome photo of the company's CEO and his vital statistics (age, salary, golf handicap, number of employees axed, etc.). I've also included a little background on the company's "crimes," which I define as any lawbreaking (civil or criminal) or other activities that we should definitely *consider* illegal or immoral.

I hope you enjoy these cards. Pass 'em around to your friends, give 'em to your kids, take 'em to the ballpark.

Maybe we can start a new national pastime!

WILLIAM S. STAVROPOULOS is president and chief executive officer of Dow Chemical Company, having assumed this post in November 1995. He became president and chief operating officer in 1993, senior vice president in 1991, vice president in 1990, and has held other senior posts since the 1980s. "Stav" became Dow U.S.A.'s president in 1990 and a board member of Dow Corning in March 1991.

We know Dow best through its household products, such as Fantastik, Saran Wrap, Spray 'N' Wash, and Ziploc bags. But did you also know that Dow is the world's largest producer of chlorine (about 40 million tons each year), which generates dioxin, the most toxic synthetic chemical known to science? In fact, Dow is probably the world's largest root dioxin source, according to Greenpeace (although the company denies this). Dioxin is an extremely potent carcinogen that also affects reproduction, child development, and the immune system.

During and before Vietnam, Dow became the largest U.S. supplier of 2,4,5-T, the active component of Agent Orange. But while that and other pesticides were restricted in the 1980s, Dow continues to make other dioxin-contaminated pesticides to this day.

In 1995, Dow paid $167,339 in Environmental Protection Agency (EPA) fines for hazardous waste violations at its plant in Midland, Michigan, according to the Council on Economic Priorities.

Also in 1995, the EPA fined DowElanco $876,000. Dow-Elanco is a joint venture between Dow Chemical and Eli Lilly. It seems the company failed to report information on the adverse health effects of a number of its pesticides, including Dursban, the country's leading termite-control brand.

Dow Chemical is also 50 percent owner of Dow Corning, which was the leading maker of breast implants and silicone gel. In October 1995, a Nevada jury hit Dow Chemical with

CORPORATE Crook #1
DOW CHEMICAL CO.
William S. Stavropoulos, President and CEO

Personal goals: hopes thinned-out management ranks at Dow can relate to workers as "their coach, their teammate, their adviser"

Quote: "[T]he buck truly stops at the CEO's level."

Headquarters: Midland, Michigan
Nickname: Stav or Bill
Age: 56
Annual compensation: $1.28 million including salary and bonus
Born: Bridgehampton, Long Island
Education: B.A. in pharmaceutical chemistry, Fordham University, 1961; Ph.D. in medicinal chemistry, University of Washington, 1966
Years with company: 29
Jobs eliminated since 1993: 15,800
Affiliations: Midland Country Club (Dow Club); board member American Plastics Council, Chemical Bank, Chemical Manufacturers Association
Height: 6'1"
Eyes: brown
Hair color: brownish silver
Throws: right
Bats: right
Drives: Cadillac FTS
Leisure-time activities: baseball fan and childhood friend of Hall of Famer Carl Yastrzemski

a $14.1 million verdict in a breast implant case. According to the plaintiff's lawyers, "Dow Chemical knew early on about the dangers of liquid silicone and concealed them from the public." Dow has appealed the verdict and denies that breast implants cause disease of any kind.

• • •

DAVID H. HOAG has been chairman, president, and CEO of LTV Steel since 1991, and has been in senior posts since 1986, when he was appointed executive vice president for

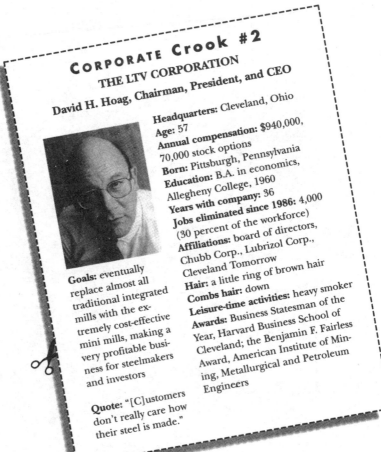

CORPORATE Crook #2
THE LTV CORPORATION
David H. Hoag, Chairman, President, and CEO

Headquarters: Cleveland, Ohio
Age: 57
Annual compensation: $940,000, 70,000 stock options
Born: Pittsburgh, Pennsylvania
Education: B.A. in economics, Allegheny College, 1960
Years with company: 36
Jobs eliminated since 1986: 4,000 (30 percent of the workforce)
Affiliations: board of directors, Chubb Corp., Lubrizol Corp., Cleveland Tomorrow
Hair: a little ring of brown hair
Combs hair: down
Leisure-time activities: heavy smoker
Awards: Business Statesman of the Year, Harvard Business School of Cleveland; the Benjamin F. Fairless Award, American Institute of Mining, Metallurgical and Petroleum Engineers

Goals: eventually replace almost all traditional integrated mills with the extremely cost-effective mini mills, making a very profitable business for steelmakers and investors

Quote: "[C]ustomers don't really care how their steel is made."

steel and elected to the board. This Cleveland-based company (with offices in Mexico and Japan) is the nation's third-largest steel company. GM is its largest customer (11 percent of revenues).

LTV went bankrupt in 1986. Desperate to get the company out of bankruptcy, the workers and the city of Cleveland gave the company huge concessions, including a ten-year tax abatement plan from the city.

As a result, the company recovered from bankruptcy in 1993 and once again became profitable. But it did not use these new profits to return something to the workers and the community, such as expanding or improving their existing facilities. Instead, it decided to build a *new* steel minimill (employing far fewer workers) in Decatur, Alabama (a joint venture with two foreign companies, dubbed Trico). This was after extracting from Alabama over $85 million in *additional* state tax subsidies and $250 million in assistance from the city of Decatur.

At this point it's unclear whether the plant will even be union. Says Cleveland steelworker Mike Scarver, "When no one else would help LTV, when the financial institutions turned their back, we helped them. . . . LTV should put that money back into the communities that cared about LTV surviving."

As we go to press, taking money from one community and building new plants in another one is not a crime, just "good business."

• • •

Nike was founded in 1968 by **PHIL KNIGHT,** chairman, CEO, and owner of about 35 percent of Nike's stock. Nike is the world's biggest shoe company. Nike spent a reported $250 million on advertising in 1994. Net income for 1995 was nearly $400 million.

Nike itself makes very few shoes; the company buys its shoes mostly from Asian contractors. According to a September 1994 report by Netherlands-based IRENE (International Restructuring Education Network Europe), 99 percent of the 90 million shoes Nike sells every year are produced in Asia, by a contractor workforce of over 75,000.

Thirty-six percent of Nike's shoes are manufactured in Indonesia, notorious for human rights abuses and poor working conditions. Indonesian girls and young women who sew the shoes start at an entry-level rate of about two dollars a day, a wage that meets only two-thirds of workers' "basic physical needs," as defined by the Indonesian government. Compulsory overtime, which is against Indonesian law, is common, as are other violations concerning working hours and holidays, maternity leave, and health and safety. One labor organizer who visited Indonesia found at least three of the Nike contractors using child labor, with one fourteen-year-old girl sewing shoes for fifty hours a week. Physical attacks on workers occur often.

Nike denies these conditions exist. It says the company adopted a voluntary code of conduct in 1992, entering into "memorandums of understanding" with each of its suppliers to ensure that they upheld Nike standards. But Nike contractors' current activities in Indonesia appear to violate the company's code.

And what about doing business with a country like Indonesia, which suppresses strikes, posts military personnel at factory offices, and frequently jails labor leaders? The Indonesian military has killed approximately 200,000 people in East Timor, about one-third of its population. Nike relies on U.S. support of the Indonesian government, which provides the political protection they need to keep their factories operating.

Nike pays Michael Jordan $20 million a year in endorsement fees. This fee exceeded the entire annual payroll of the Indonesian factories that make the shoes. According to other press reports, Andre Agassi has agreed to a ten-year, $100 million contract to endorse Nike products. It would take 1 percent of Nike's entire advertising budget to put its whole workforce of 12,000 above the poverty line.

CORPORATE Crook #3

NIKE, INC.

Philip H. Knight, Founder, Owner, Chairman, and CEO

Headquarters: Beaverton, Oregon
Nickname: Phil
Age: 58
Annual compensation: $1,678,000
Born: Portland, Oregon
Education: B.B.A., University of Oregon, 1959; M.B.A., Stanford, 1962; C.P.A., Oregon
Years with company: 28
Workers fired in U.S.: closed manufacturing plants in U.S. in the mid-1980s, firing over 2,000 workers
Affiliations: a couple of local golf clubs he doesn't have time to play at very often; Episcopal Church; Republican Party; American International CPAs
Height: 5'11"
Weight: 170 pounds
Eyes: blue
Hair: lots of curly blond/gray
Combs hair: doesn't
Bats: right
Throws: right
Car: Acura NSX
Golf handicap: 8
Leisure-time activities: avid runner, tennis player, reader, bookstore browser

One redeeming quality: contributed $25,000 to Tonya Harding's legal fund

Quote: "We can't take our eye off the ball, because if we lose it, we'll have a bitch of a time getting it back."

Proud accomplishment: more than 90 speeding tickets

RALPH S. LARSEN has been chairman, CEO, and president of Johnson & Johnson since 1989. He was vice chairman of Johnson & Johnson's board of directors from 1986 to 1989, and company group chairman from 1985 to 1986.

Between 1985 and 1988, the Ortho Pharmaceutical Corporation, a wholly owned subsidiary of Johnson & Johnson, began a public relations campaign to promote the acne medication Retin-A to treat sun-wrinkled skin, a use for which the FDA had not approved it. In January 1991, the Justice Department served a grand jury subpoena on Johnson & Johnson and Ortho relating to this PR campaign. At

CORPORATE Crook #4
ORTHO PHARMACEUTICAL CO.
(Wholly owned by Johnson & Johnson)
Ralph S. Larsen, Chairman, President, and CEO

Headquarters: New Brunswick, New Jersey
Age: 57
Annual compensation: $2,675,000
Born: Brooklyn, New York
Education: B.B.A., Hofstra University, 1962
Years with company: 34
Workers fired since becoming CEO: at least 3,600
Affiliations: board member, Xerox Corp., New York Stock Exchange, and AT&T; vice chairman of the Business Council
Eyes: blue
Hair: a little white hair
Combs hair: to the right, over the bald spot
Leisure-time activities: downhill and cross-country skiing, modern art
Hero figure: Winston Churchill, "for his ability to do what's right under adversity"

Quote: "We will not willingly give up one [market] share point to anybody."

that point, Ortho officials persuaded employees to destroy thousands of relevant documents and hide videotapes.

In January 1995, Ortho pleaded guilty to obstruction of justice by persuading employees to destroy documents and was fined $5 million and ordered to pay $2.5 million in restitution. The federal judge said that "Ortho destroyed its records hoping that the full truth would never be known," and that destruction of records "did not take place in a vacuum."

In addition, in October 1995, the Johnson & Johnson consumer division settled Federal Trade Commission charges that, in order to promote its spermicidal jelly K-Y PLUS Nonoxynol-9, it made false advertising claims that exaggerated the failure rate of condoms.

In 1995, the *Multinational Monitor* named Johnson & Johnson one of the ten worst corporations because of Ortho's misconduct.

• • •

JAN D. TIMMER has been president of Philips Electronics, based in the Netherlands, since 1990. He'll be retiring at the end of 1996. In 1977, Timmer was appointed chief executive, Philips South Africa. Philips is best known for its consumer electronics and for its multimedia subsidiary, PolyGram (distributor of my film *Canadian Bacon*).

In June 1995, North American Philips, a division of Philips and one of the world's largest producers of semiconductors and electronic components, pleaded guilty to defrauding the Department of Defense. The company had falsified and destroyed DOD records at its plant in Mineral Wells, Texas. The falsified testing data concerned military equipment for the Defense Department and the National Aeronautics and Space Administration (NASA). The destroyed data indicated that Defense Department standards were not being met.

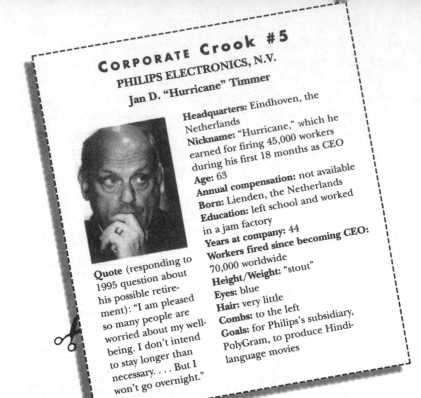

CORPORATE Crook #5

PHILIPS ELECTRONICS, N.V.

Jan D. "Hurricane" Timmer

Headquarters: Eindhoven, the Netherlands
Nickname: "Hurricane," which he earned for firing 45,000 workers during his first 18 months as CEO
Age: 63
Annual compensation: not available
Born: Lienden, the Netherlands
Education: left school and worked in a jam factory
Years at company: 44
Workers fired since becoming CEO: 70,000 worldwide
Height/Weight: "stout"
Eyes: blue
Hair: very little
Combs: to the left
Goals: for Philips's subsidiary, PolyGram, to produce Hindi-language movies

Quote (responding to 1995 question about his possible retirement): "I am pleased so many people are worried about my well-being. I don't intend to stay longer than necessary. . . . But I won't go overnight."

The company agreed to deposit $9 million toward customer claims involving its Mineral Wells plant and place another $5 million in an escrow account toward nongovernmental claims. But don't expect much of a "deterrent" effect. Jon Kasle, a spokesman for Philips, told *The New York Times,* "This is not a big deal for a $34 billion company."

Until January 1991, Philips's Mineral Wells facility manufactured approximately 40 percent of the military specification resistors used by NASA and the Pentagon in communications, navigation, and weapons systems, such as the Air Force F-16 Fighting Falcon, the U.S. Army Patriot missile, and the Global Positioning Satellite System.

The Mineral Wells plant is now being closed.

Keun Hee Lee is the CEO and chairman of South Korea's biggest conglomerate, Samsung Group. He's been chairman since 1987. The company was founded by Lee's father in 1938 as a small rice shop. Last year, sales totaled $75 billion. Lee and his family have a controlling stake in the company and a fortune that *Forbes* estimates at $4 billion.

In 1992, Samsung's U.S. subsidiary, Samsung America, made $10,000 in illegal corporate campaign contributions

CORPORATE Crook #6
SAMSUNG
Keun Hee Lee, Chairman and CEO

Headquarters: Seoul, Korea
Age: 54
Annual compensation: not available
Born: Taegu, Korea
Education: B.A., Waseda University, Japan, 1965; M.B.A., George Washington University, Washington, D.C., 1966
Years with company: 30
Affiliations: chairman, Korean Amateur Wrestling Association; cochair, Korean Olympic Organizing Committee
Eyes: brown
Hair: black
Combs hair: to the right
Bats: right
Throws: right
Drives: Porsche 911
Golf handicap: 14–15
Leisure-time activities: horseback riding, golf, Ping-Pong, playing with his couple hundred dogs, "200 mph jaunts down the German Autobahn"
Biggest faux pas: Turned off Steven Spielberg at dinner. He was there to finalize a deal with the DreamWorks Studio, but used the word *semiconductor* so many times they decided they didn't want his money.

Goals: for Samsung's annual sales to reach $200 billion, more than any company in the world

One redeeming quality: works to protect animals, including saving mongrels from becoming "food dogs"

to Representative Jay C. Kim (R-Calif.), the first Korean American elected to Congress. It is illegal for corporations and foreigners to contribute to federal election campaigns.

In February 1996, Samsung America pleaded guilty in federal court to making these contributions through five southern California–based employees and their wives. The company paid a $150,000 fine. In exchange for Samsung America's guilty plea, the federal government agreed to end its investigation of more serious crimes, including obstruction of justice, conspiracy, and mail fraud by the company and its employees.

Meanwhile, in South Korea, Chairman Lee, along with eight other South Korean business tycoons, is being prosecuted for allegedly bribing South Korea's former president Roh Tae Woo in order to obtain government contracts. In January, prosecutors asked for a jail sentence for Lee—although this is unlikely.

In 1995, the Occupational Safety and Health Administration (OSHA) cited Samsung Guam, another Samsung subsidiary, for 118 willful violations during the expansion of the Guam International Air Terminal. OSHA said that for six months the company ignored obvious fall hazards, resulting in serious accidents and the death of one welder, who fell fifty-one feet while working on a roof overhang. The proposed $8.2 million penalty is a record for the construction industry.

• • •

WILLIAM RUTLEDGE has been chairman of Teledyne, Inc., since 1993, CEO since 1991, and president since 1990. Between 1986 and 1990 he held various vice-presidential positions with the company. Teledyne is a Los Angeles–based defense contractor.

In 1995, Teledyne pleaded guilty to violating the U.S.

Arms Export Control Act by illegally exporting enough weapons-grade zirconium—130 tons—to make 24,000 cluster bombs. Teledyne's customer was Chilean arms maker Carlos Cardoen, who allegedly sold at least ten thousand cluster bombs to Iraq in the 1980s during the Iran-Iraq war, according to the Associated Press. Cluster bombs explode in the air and release fiery bomblets that cover a wide range. At least one of the bombs turned up in an Iraqi bunker during the Gulf War.

CORPORATE Crook #7

TELEDYNE, INC.

William Rutledge, Chairman, President, and CEO

Quote (responding to suggestions that Teledyne has a pattern of corruption): "[That's] completely absurd and frankly is offensive in the worst way."

Goal: to increase "absolutely unacceptable" profits, due to legal expenses, excessive operating costs, and the economy

Headquarters: Los Angeles, California
Age: 54
Annual compensation: $1,065,500
Education: B.S. in metallurgical engineering, Lafayette College, 1963; M.S. in financial management, George Washington University; Stanford Executive Program, 1984
Years with company: 10
Jobs eliminated since becoming CEO: at least 3,000
Affiliations: board member, First Federal Bank of California (a Los Angeles S&L)
Eyes: blue
Hair: white
Combs hair: to the right
Author: "Noncontracting Strip Tension System Provides Tight Coils" in the February 1971 edition of *Iron and Steel Engineer*
Proudest accomplishment at old job: building a tank/troop carrier to fight the Russians, which was so fast that troops returning from the testing range were given a ticket for exceeding the 35 mph speed limit

The judge prevented Teledyne from defending itself by blaming the Bush and Reagan administrations, which it said "winked" at arms sales by Cardoen to Iraq.

Also in 1995, Teledyne settled for $2.2 million a claim originally brought by a whistle-blower, which alleged that Teledyne harassed this employee into quitting after he told investigators that between 1984 and 1994 the company was using falsified tests to sell substandard radio gear to the U.S. government. Employees had been instructed to fake tests of electronic gadgets on Stinger and other missiles that enable U.S. soldiers to distinguish friendly from enemy aircraft, so they know which ones to shoot down. About 2,500 components that failed tests were sold to the military.

The government's investigation into this matter led to several civil cases, forcing the company to pay more than $19 million in settlements. Teledyne denies any wrongdoing, so don't expect much deterrent effect as a result of these settlements. In addition, in 1994, the company settled two whistle-blower suits for $112.5 million, dealing with both the falsified tests and padding estimates on government contracts.

In 1993, the Pentagon banned one of Teledyne's subsidiaries from receiving government contracts for a year because the company pleaded guilty to improperly testing nine million electronic components for a variety of weapons. This was the first time the Pentagon had ever imposed so strong a sanction against one of its hundred largest contractors, according to the *Los Angeles Times*. Also in 1993, Teledyne agreed to pay $2.15 million to settle claims brought by a former quality assurance engineer that the company's controls division falsified tests on cockpit electronics systems. And in 1992, Teledyne paid a $17.5 million criminal fine for defense fraud involving Teledyne Relays false tests—at the time the largest settlement ever in a criminal defense fraud case.

Where's the "three strikes and you're out" provision when it comes to corporate crime?

• • •

MELVIN R. GOODES is chairman and CEO of Warner-Lambert, the New Jersey–based drug giant that makes the Parke-Davis line of drugs (Benadryl, Listerine, Halls cough drops). He's held this position since 1991. Between 1985

CORPORATE Crook #8
WARNER-LAMBERT CO.
Melvin R. Goodes, Chairman and CEO

Headquarters: Morris Plains, New Jersey

Age: 61

Annual compensation: $1,722,000

Born: Hamilton, Ontario

Education: B.Commerce, Queens University, Kingston, Ontario, 1957; M.B.A., University of Chicago, 1960

Years with company: 31

Workers fired since becoming CEO: good news—work force has increased by 3,000; bad news— 5,500 jobs targeted for elimination

Affiliations: Plainfield Golf Club, Pine Valley Golf Club

Eyes: blue

Hair: more than usual for a CEO

Combs hair: to the left

Bats: right

Throws: right

Car: Jaguar (used to drive "His and Hers," but "Hers" left)

Golf handicap: 10

Favorite club on the fairway: driver, likes to hit the ball long

Leisure-time activities: tennis, Rotisserie Basketball League, golf nut

Quote: "I've teed off when it's 15 degrees out. It's nothing to me. I'm Canadian."

Quote: "Contingency work can provide the flexible job opportunities many people are looking for."

and 1991, he was president and chief operating officer of the company.

From 1990 to 1993, the company hid from the Food and Drug Administration flawed manufacturing processes it had used for several drugs, including Dilantin, a popular epilepsy treatment, and three other drugs no longer made by the company that had been used to treat Parkinson's disease and thyroid conditions. As a result, drugs were not stable chemically and lost their potency. Many patients may have received dosages that were less than intended.

In 1993, the company had agreed to stop much of its drug production, including that of its popular antacid, Rolaids, while improving its manufacturing processes. No more flawed drugs should have been shipped after that time. But according to the U.S. Attorney, since then Warner-Lambert's own tests demonstrated that the drugs were unstable.

In November 1995, the company pleaded guilty to a felony and agreed to pay a $10 million fine for covering up these problems. Even though this was the largest FDA fine ever levied on a brand-name drug company, it's barely a dent in the company's $700 million net income. Even securities analysts characterized the fine as "minor."

Why Are Union Leaders So F#!@ing Stupid?

CAN YOU THINK of a more embarrassing sight than what passes for a union leader these days? These guys are the most pathetic bunch of losers I've seen since my ninth-grade remedial metal shop class.

I am convinced that, hundreds of years from now, when anthropologists dig up the remnants of our culture and study our behavior, they will not be able to figure out why most of the leaders of our major labor unions rolled over and let the company bosses destroy the lives of their members.

"Just how friggin' stupid were these guys?" the social scientists of the twenty-third century will wonder in amazement. Should these future Americans run across a copy of this book, allow me to explain just how stupid.

Douglas Fraser of the United Auto

Workers was so stupid that, when he was president of the union in the early eighties, he accepted a seat on the Chrysler board of directors so he could be a "watchdog on the board." While Fraser was watchdogging on behalf of his union, Chrysler closed twenty factories and three parts depots, eventually firing more than 50,000 people! Remind me never to ask this guy to watch my house while I'm away.

The next president of the UAW, Owen Bieber, was so stupid that, in 1987, he signed an "attrition agreement" with General Motors. For every two people who retired, died, or quit, GM would only have to replace *one* of them. Bieber decided it was better to *decrease* the membership of his union and then have the remaining members working faster, harder, and longer than ever before. The year he agreed to this, GM was already making a profit of $3.6 billion.

The leadership of the Communications Workers of America was so stupid that, in 1992, they agreed to let AT&T start a "Workplace of the Future" program in which labor and management would work "more closely together" in teams, instead of in the traditional "confrontational" mode. The next year, AT&T closed forty regional centers and eliminated 4,000 jobs. After six more months of "cooperation," AT&T cut 15,000 more jobs. The union still didn't want to dissolve the "team"—and so, a year later, AT&T announced it was firing another 40,000 employees! Only then did it dawn on the union leaders that AT&T was up to something.

Other union leaders have also stupidly fallen for this trend of "cooperation" with management called "Quality of Work Life." It is nothing more than an effort to find new ways to eliminate jobs and bust unions.

In another blast of official union stupidity, Lane Kirkland, the recently dethroned head of the AFL-CIO, decided that the best way to oppose the North American Free Trade Agreement was to do so by quietly lobbying Congress. So along came Ross Perot and Pat Buchanan to fill his void and spearhead a very public movement against NAFTA. By stupidly surrendering the issue to these two nutcases, Kirkland allowed Clinton to appear rational, and the President was able to get NAFTA passed.

Union leaders are so stupid that, since the late seventies, they have continually agreed to cut their members' wages and benefits *simply because the company asked them to!* The companies have taken the newfound savings, and instead of creating more jobs in the United States, they've built new plants overseas, resulting in the firing of the very American workers who gave them that money!

In my hometown of Flint, Michigan, the UAW leadership was so stupid that they actively lobbied the city council to grant General Motors tax abatements that, over the last twenty years, have given them tax breaks on $1.8 billion worth of property. They did so because they believed GM would create new jobs if given the tax breaks. Instead, GM eliminated more than 40,000 jobs in that period in Flint—and hasn't given a dime of its tax savings back to the city.

The list of Union Leadership Stupidity could fill the rest of this book. It is sad for me, on a personal level, even to have to write this chapter. My uncle Laverne participated in the Great Flint Sit Down Strike of 1936–37, which resulted in the first contract for the United Auto Workers and was, as historians have written, the beginning of the modern-day labor movement across America. Because of what my uncle and others fought for over the years, families like mine were able to live in homes that we owned, go to a doctor whenever we were sick, get our teeth fixed whenever they needed it, or go to college if we chose to—all thanks to the union.

This progress all came to an end on August 5, 1981, when President Ronald Reagan fired 11,400 striking air traffic control workers and permanently replaced them, an event unheard of in U.S. history. From that day on, the union movement has been on a downward slide to oblivion. Labor union leaders, in the stupidest moment in their history, refused to call for a general, nationwide strike that would have shut the country down until Reagan rehired the controllers. Union members crossed picket lines and continued to fly. I remember refusing to get on a plane for the next eight months—and having a hard time walking from New York to L.A. and persuading others to do likewise. So I gave up and started to fly.

Reagan broke the air traffic controllers' union, which, in their own stupidity, had endorsed him in the election, thinking they would get the best deal with Ronnie in the Oval Office! Stupid. Stupid. Stupid. Reagan became a hero to big business—which then went on a tear throughout the rest of the decade, smashing unions, making record profits, copping huge tax breaks, and tripling the national deficit. Reagan and company were able to get away with this because they knew labor would not challenge them on any of it.

And that's exactly what happened. Our labor leaders all should have changed their names to Neville Chamberlain (the Brit who rolled over to Hitler in 1938). Instead of fighting back—*hard*—our union leaders let the right wing and corporate honchos take our country away from us, without a peep from anyone in labor.

Here, in essence, was labor's response to Corporate America's downsizing:

"Yes, sir, General Motors, you want to close these factories and move them to Mexico? No problem! How can we help you? You say you don't want to pay your corporate taxes? No problem! You don't have to pay *any!* So you want five of us workers to do the same exact job it used to take ten workers to do? Happy to oblige! No, we don't mind working seven days a week! Why give jobs to the unemployed when we can just work longer hours ourselves? We don't need to see our kids! You want us to blame the Japanese for taking our jobs? Hey, that's easy! Gimme a sledgehammer and a foreign car to bash! Heck, just give me a foreigner to bash! I'll have no trouble venting my anger against the enemy you've created for me! Better them than you!"

Our labor leaders seem to have forgotten an important lesson we learned in elementary school: if you give the bully what the bully wants, the bully doesn't become your friend—he just wants more *because he knows he can get it!* The only way you stopped the bully back in school was to stand up to him and face him down. Even if he did end up kicking your ass, he suddenly had a newfound respect for you that he didn't have for the others who appeased him. He would generally leave you alone after that, because it was too much trouble to have to wrestle you down and wash your face in the snow. It was easier just to move on to the others who would give him what he wanted.

Life in the work world is not that much different. When the early unionists stood up to the companies, it resulted in a higher standard of living for all of us—even for those who didn't belong to a union. Thanks to labor unions, we have social security, Medicare and Medicaid, child labor laws, safety standards, and wages that allow even the most unskilled worker to purchase many products—which, in turn, gives more people jobs.

Those of you who like to say nasty things about unions should look around and see how much better your life is because somebody else *in a union* fought for those things. Businesses will never do the right thing unless they are forced to.

So what happened to our union leaders? Why did they go soft? Did they get too accustomed to their $100,000-a-year jobs and plush offices, forgetting where they came from? Or did we, as union members, forget our responsibility to remain vigilant? Decades ago, monthly meetings at the union halls were packed. By the mid-1980s, you could barely get a quorum. People were too busy voting for Reagan and Bush. Or maybe we were just enjoying all those creature comforts that our union paychecks bought that we forgot to put down the remote control to our big-screen TV, get off the couch, and get down to the union meeting.

How many of us even know who our union leaders are? As I sit here today, a member of three different unions (the Writers Guild, the Directors Guild, and AFTRA), I cannot tell you the name of the president of any of my unions. If yours truly, Mr. Big Time Pro-Labor Guy, doesn't even know that simple information, it isn't hard to understand how we have all fallen asleep at the wheel.

I've come to the conclusion that, instead of carping about the jerks who run our unions, maybe I should do something myself to help save the labor movement in my own small way.

Producing this book, as I've discovered, has turned out to be a nonunion affair. Crown Publishers, Inc., and its parent, Random House, are nonunion. The people who edit this book are not represented by a union. The guy who designed the jacket has no union affiliation. The printers Random House uses are also nonunion, as is the warehouse that distributes the books. I spoke with many of these individuals in an attempt to get them to join a union. They were at least polite as they tried not to roll their eyes. Only the paper that was milled for these pages and the cover of this book was produced by union labor.

I, myself, have hired two individuals who are doing research for me on this book. Their names are Gillian Aldrich and Tia Lessin. Neither belongs to a union. Now, I know, you're saying, "Hey, Mike, your workers don't need a union! I'll bet your office is a really cool place to work, a nonstop rock-'n'-roll party for the proletariat!"

Right, except for one thing: they do not own this book, will not share in its potential profits, must work long hours, and can be let go at any time. They have no protection, and no matter what a nice guy I've convinced myself that I am, they are at my mercy. Unless they are equity owners in this project, I have the up position, and their work lives are controlled by my whims.

That's why Tia and Gillian and all workers need representation. Think of it as an equalizer. We live in a country that's founded on the basic principle of fairness: that all people should be treated with dignity and should have a say in the matters that affect their lives. Why do we abandon this principle when we enter the office door? Isn't this America, too? Or is "life, liberty and the pursuit of happiness" not allowed from 9 to 5?

So I've begun a movement to organize this book. Two months ago I encouraged Tia and Gillian to find a union they would want to join and told them I would recognize it and enter into a contract with them. They seemed excited by this prospect (some would say a little *too* excited) and began their organizing drive.

What they've discovered during these past few months speaks volumes about everything that's wrong with organized labor these days.

First they called the Writers Guild—thinking, rightly, "Hey, this is a book." So a writers' union would be a natural. The Writers Guild told them, "Sorry, we don't represent workers in the book industry—only writers in radio, TV, and film." The receptionist suggested they call the Authors Guild.

So they called the Authors Guild. They were told that the Authors Guild isn't really a union—"We just provide members with legal advice and stuff like that." They suggested Tia and Gillian call the Association of American Publishers.

Of course, the AAP is the anti-union—it's the group that represents management and owners in the publishing world.

A friend of Tia's suggested the National Writers Union. I had heard of them and they sounded like a good group of progressive folks. But when Tia called the office of the New York local, at two o'clock on a Monday afternoon, all she got was an answering machine. She left a message saying she urgently needed to join a union. It's been four months and she still hasn't heard from them.

Feeling exasperated, they decided to call the Brooklyn local of the seafarers' union. They explained that they both "loved the water," and each of them owned a blue striped T-shirt. They spoke with the "port agent," who told them they had to get "seaman's papers," and the only way to do that was to apply to the Coast Guard.

Tia called the Coast Guard—but there was no answer. So much for national security.

Next up was the longshoremen's union. The guy there told them to get papers first from the Waterfront Commission. But the man at the Waterfront Commission told them they don't issue papers anymore to anybody—"not even [New York City Mayor] Giuliani himself." I guess that means nobody.

Their next call went to the machinists' union (Tia and Gillian have to keep fixing the fax machine here in the office, so we thought they would qualify as machinists). The union seemed interested, but said the women would have to fork over a $300 initiation fee. That's a month's worth of groceries.

So it was on to other unions. Tia called the sanitation workers' union. The representative asked her which trash company she worked for.

"Random House," she replied.

"That's not a trash company," he said.

"Yes, it is. They publish Joan Collins."

"Our rules are very specific. You have to *pick up* trash, not put it out."

He did refer her to Teamster locals 1034 and 840—the miscellaneous locals that cover hay-and-feed workers at the racetrack, cemetery groundskeepers, and needle workers at the blood bank. Finally she was getting somewhere.

The people at Teamster local 840 were more than happy to sign Tia and Gillian up. All that was left was for me to sit down and negotiate the contract.

But the process of finding a union had taken so long that I did not speak to the union rep until Tia had finished her work on the book. Gillian will be staying to work on the book tour, so she will be represented by the Teamsters.

That's one down, 108,800,000 nonunionized workers to go. No problem! As labor historian Peter Rachleff pointed out recently in *The Nation*, back in the 1920s, unions went from representing nearly 20 percent of the country's work-force down to almost 10 percent. Unions looked like they were finished. At that time, like today, the wealthy 1 percent earned more than the entire combined income of the bottom 40 percent. Strikes had become a thing of the past, and labor leaders urged the rank and file to "act with caution and to cooperate with management." Wages became stagnant, the work week lengthened, and Wall Street was giddy with investors.

But eventually, the chickens came home to roost. The stock market crashed, and within ten years, millions of Americans had gone on strike and formed new and bigger unions. Life got better. It can again.

And this time, with so many white-collar workers and managers being downsized, we'll soon have the chance to see our former bosses marching with us in solidarity on the picket line. Whatever hardships we've all been going through !ately, it will have been worth it just to see that day!

Balance the Budget?
Balance My Checkbook!

THE CLUELESS AWARD for the 1996 election year has to go to Bob Dole. Still in shock the day after losing to Pat Buchanan in the New Hampshire primary, Dole said he didn't realize that jobs and the economy were that important to the voters. Whoa! Next!

Bob had spent the better part of the previous year making a balanced federal budget the top priority in Congress. In the symbolic last vote he called for on the Senate floor before resigning, Dole demanded a balanced budget amendment to the Constitution. Twice before, he and his fellow Republicans shut down the federal government, feeling assured that the American people would rally behind their battle cry, BALANCE THE BUDGET!

Whoops. Big mistake. The American

CHAPTER 17

public couldn't give a rat's ass about a federal balanced budget *because they're too damn busy trying to balance their own!* Dole was shocked that the American people were so distraught over NAFTA and the other little ditties that have cost them their jobs. Where has this guy been?

The debate over balancing the federal budget—one that Clinton foolishly joined in on—is nothing but a distraction, an attempt by the politicians to get our minds off the real problems in our country. Are they really so stupid as to think we give a damn about the deficit? What about *our* deficit?

The average working American earns about $14,420 a year. The average household has a yearly income of about $30,000—and carries a debt of $33,000. That's a deficit of $3,000. The average person these days does not have a balanced budget. The total consumer debt in America is just under $5 trillion—virtually the same amount as the federal debt!

These are not easy times. People live from paycheck to paycheck. Many don't even bother balancing their checkbooks because what's the point? There *is* no balance!

Take a look at the monthly budget of anyone, and it'll prove my point.

Take Bob and Debbie Davis of San Diego, California. They are friends of my sister Veronica. They have two kids and a combined income of $48,444 a year—and they are unable to balance their budget. Something is very wrong with the country when a family cannot survive on $48,000 a year. Let's take a look at how the Davises try to get by.

Bob and Debbie both have college degrees. Bob is a recreational therapist working with impaired children at a San Diego hospital. Debbie is a teacher but cannot find a full-time job. The school district hires her for 3.75 hours a day as a permanent substitute—just under the minimum of four hours that would require them to pay her benefits. Together, after taxes, their net monthly income is $2,982.

Their total expenses? $3,490—$500 more than what they take in.

And what kind of extravagant lifestyle are Bob and Debbie living? They drive a ten-year-old and a five-year-old Honda. They rent a seventy-year-old house from their relative who gives them a break on the rent. Their dining out consists of going out for Mexican fast food once a week. Luxuries? They send the girls to dance class. Oh, and they have cable. And, like most working people, they give a greater percentage of their income to charity than do the rich (in the Davises' case, to the Sierra Club, Mothers Against Drunk Driving, Girl Scouts, and Children's Hospital).

Yet they are barely getting by, carrying at least $5,000 in debt on their Visa and paying 14 percent in overdraft charges to the credit union to cover expenses between paychecks. Between groceries, clothes, constantly fixing the aging cars, gasoline, utilities, house insurance, auto insurance, school supplies, school and work lunches, phone bills (never over $30 a month), and the deductibles on Bob's health insurance, they find themselves in the hole each month. Unlike their parents, who worked in the aerospace and insurance industries, Bob and Debbie Davis, hardworking Americans, will not live the American Dream their parents had hoped to pass on to them.

We live in an economic system that not only encourages debt, but demands it. If we weren't willing to take out loans and pay huge financing charges to banks, those institutions would go under. If we didn't have credit cards so we could go to stores and buy things we can't afford, those stores would go under. Without us living our lives in perpetual debt, the system would collapse. Want a house? Take out a loan, go into debt! Want a car? Take out a loan, go into debt!

If you don't go into debt, the system punishes you. The first used car I bought, I paid cash. A few years later, when I wanted to buy a new car, I couldn't get a loan because I had no "debt history." I was punished for keeping a balanced budget! Only when I went into debt—my credit union was obligated under its charter to grant me the car loan—was I then accepted by the system. I have never had trouble going into debt again.

The same thing happens with credit cards. The more you spend—and go into debt—the more credit cards they send you. If you spend over your credit limit, do they punish you? No! They call you and tell you your credit limit has been raised another $5,000—"so spend away!" And we do.

I find it pretty crazy that senators in D.C. are telling us that the main priority on our political agenda should be a balanced federal budget. If we can't live with one in our personal lives, they should wise up and realize that we don't give a damn about "their" budget until they start giving a damn about ours.

So quit closing down the federal government—we don't want our parents calling us to send cash 'cause their Social Security checks haven't arrived (except you, Mom and Dad. You can call anytime).

And quit carrying on about a balanced budget. We just don't care, because we can't care.

> "We have a captive labor force, a group of men who are dedicated, who want to work. That makes the whole business profitable."
>
> —Bob Tessler, owner of a company that contracts for prison labor

Mike's Penal Systems, Inc.

PROSPECTUS

AN OFFERING

CHAPTER 18

MIKE'S PENAL SYSTEMS, INC., is offering 1 million shares of common stock at twenty-five dollars per share and a stake in the most exciting and profitable growth industry in America—private prisons!

These proceeds will be used for Mike's Penal Systems, Inc. (known hereafter as "MPS, Inc."), which will provide a unique service that benefits both the shareholders and the community. In addition to building and operating private prisons, MPS, Inc., will join with the many other private and public prisons in the country that have contracted with major U.S. corporations to provide inexpensive prison labor in the production of goods and services.

The common stock offered hereby involves a low degree of risk, as there is no way we'll run out of inmates anywhere in America in the near future.

BACKGROUND

In the past fifteen years the U.S. prison population has tripled. There are now more than 1.5 million prison beds in the United States. The cost to the government is over $15,000 a year per inmate.

Recently, private prison companies have decided they could offer the same services to the government, but at a lower cost—and make significant profits at the same time.

Today, more than 65,000 inmates are in private sector prisons. Investors such as American Express and Smith Barney have already seen the advantage of investing in the private prison industry. As one investor has said, "I used to invest in hotels. But with prisons, I can guarantee 100 percent occupancy rate *every night!*"

These privatized inmates are not just sitting in their cells watching television and jerking off. They are working for many of our Fortune 500 companies—and being paid 80 percent less than the minimum wage!

In 1996 alone, according to the Reverend Jesse Jackson, $9 billion in products will be made by the private and public prison industry. American corporations will be able to downsize by approximately 400,000 jobs thanks to this savings!

THE MARKET

The potential market is unlimited. As the deindustrialization of America continues at a record rate, more and more of the workforce will be without jobs and thus thrown into a chaotic fall, spinning out of control as they attempt to save what's left of their miserable existence. As they lose their homes, cars, and life savings, many will naturally turn to crime—and thus the need for more prisons!

Because of the eroding tax base caused by companies closing facilities and moving offshore, local governments will have no choice but to rely more heavily on the private prison industry to take care of the growing criminal population. It's a win-win-win situation as long as downsizing continues as robustly as expected.

THE SUPPLIERS

The possibilities are endless when you consider the companies already using contracted prison labor to offset their costs:

TWA: Prisoners in Ventura, California, are now working as flight reservation specialists. When a customer calls the 800 number to book a flight on TWA, he or she could be talking to a convicted felon!

IBM, Texas Instruments, and Dell Computers: In Lockhart, Texas, a subcontractor, LTI, has a private prison build and fix circuit boards for these three computer giants.

AT&T: In Colorado, prisoners have worked as telemarketers for AT&T.

Microsoft: In Washington State, inmates package software and other products for Exmark, which supplies Microsoft and thirty to forty other companies.

Eddie Bauer: Also in Washington State, inmates sew fleece and Gor-Tex outdoor wear for Redwood Outdoors, which supplies companies like Eddie Bauer and Union Bay.

Spalding: Prisoners in Hawaii have worked packing and shipping Spalding golf balls.

The list goes on and on. Starbucks, Bank of America, Chevron—businesses can't move fast enough to sign up. And why not? Would you rather pay unionized employees twenty dollars an hour *plus* benefits *plus* taxes, and be forced to adhere to all of the other government regulations that go with having a noninmate workforce—just to package golf balls? Of course not!

And the added benefit of investing in Mike's Penal Systems, Inc., is that the company will guarantee that the prisoner doing this work is already pretrained—because he'll be doing the same job he had before going to the slammer—at one-tenth the cost of what he used to be paid!!

THE COMPETITION

Needless to say, smart entrepreneurs are not wasting any time getting in on the private prison market. But the possibilities are still endless, in spite of our competition:

Corrections Corporation of America: The industry leader. CCA (not to be confused with CAA, the Hollywood agents) now claims to have 48.3 percent of all the private prison business. Founded in 1983 by investors with significant holdings in Kentucky Fried Chicken, including the wife of onetime presidential candidate Lamar Alexander, CCA has grown steadily and today has forty-seven prisons in eleven states as well as Puerto Rico, Australia, and the United Kingdom.

In 1995, Corrections Corporation of America was the top growth stock among all companies based in Tennessee. Its stock rose a whopping 360.5 percent, and it was the fourth-best performer on the New York Stock Exchange.

Wackenhut: A great name for the prison business! Founded by former FBI agent George Wackenhut, the company got its start in the rent-a-cop business but later branched out into private prisons. Today, Wackenhut operates twenty-four penitentiaries in the United States, the United Kingdom, Puerto Rico, and Australia, with a total of 16,000 inmates.

Esmor: A real bottom feeder, taking the inmates *nobody wants*, including an unlimited number of sex offenders at some of its locations. Already it houses 2,500 prisoners and is expanding with deliberate speed. Esmor was featured as an "up-and-comer" in the January 1995 issue of *Forbes* magazine.

Others: Management and Training Corporation and U.S. Corrections Corporation. We are projecting that Mike's Penal Systems, Inc., will be able to overtake these small companies in the first six months.

LOCATION, LOCATION, LOCATION

Mike's Penal Systems, Inc., will target the most economically devastated areas of the country. Wherever the smokestacks are crumbling, MPS, Inc., will be there. MPS has found that those communities, with their obliterated landscapes, their desperate citizens, and their rising crime rates, are the perfect customers for MPS, Inc. Life gets real scary in places like Gary, Indiana, East St. Louis, Illinois, and Erie, Pennsylvania—and MPS, Inc., will be there to ease the fears of the law-abiding citizens by keeping the scum off the streets.

The cities with the highest crime rates last year were (in order) Atlanta, Flint, St. Louis, Tampa, Detroit, Kansas City, Newark, Little Rock, Baltimore, and Birmingham. MPS, Inc., intends to go into each of those markets in the first three years. The supply of prisoners will be endless.

These cities will also open up the vault to MPS, Inc. The company expects to receive offers of free property, 100 percent tax abatements, and federal block grants. The company anticipates paying no money for construction costs, utilities, new roads, water, sewage, or cable. State and federal programs will pay for the training of all our guards.

An added benefit will be the fact that MPS's CEO, Michael Moore, is a native of Flint, one of the Top Ten crime cities. His firsthand knowledge of this type of town will greatly enhance MPS's chances for success.

FACILITIES AND EQUIPMENT

Unlike the other private prison corporations, MPS, Inc., has no intention of building any *new* facilities. Mike's Penal Systems, Inc., will use only *existing* buildings for its penitentiaries.

All of the cities where MPS will be doing business have a number of closed factories that are perfect for not only the housing of inmates (with a few minor modifications) but the production facilities are *already in place*. Many of the inmates will be familiar with the surroundings inside the plant, since they have spent a number of years working there already!

CONTRACTORS

MPS, Inc., will not go after the "piecemeal" production business that other prison companies take on. We intend to go for the "big cheese." Why sew sweatshirts when you can build cars?

MPS will approach the top Fortune 500 companies to contract with Mike's Penal Systems for the following services:

- **Truck Assembly.** We'll have the factory, we'll have the men who used to work there—we'll build the trucks!
- **Sound Stages.** Hollywood movies need big stages and crews to shoot their films. Prisoners can build scenery *and* act as extras.
- **Medical Testing.** Prisoners are perfect specimens and often willing guinea pigs. Think of the cures we might dis-

cover with assembly-line medical experimentation! An end to AIDS—compliments of MPS, Inc.!

• **Off Premises.** Model inmates and ones nearing parole (local judges have promised to keep that number as low as possible) will be sent to work in local Toys "R" Us stores (the Toys "R" Us in Aurora, Illinois, reported much success with inmates stocking the shelves at night).

INTERNATIONAL OUTLOOK

Mike's Penal Systems, Inc., will contract with countries whose prison populations are getting to be a bit much for them to handle. China and Nigeria come to mind. MPS will bring their prisoners here to help our balance of trade and provide *totally free labor!* Other countries may be more difficult, as it is illegal in most of them to sell products produced with prison labor. But never forget that we live in an ever-changing world.

As for our most violent American criminals, MPS, Inc., will build prisons in Guatemala, Uruguay, and Jordan where the unskilled and unrehabilitated will be sent to do the type of work that U.S. regulations will not permit to be performed in this country.

A positive note: DPAS, a San Francisco–based company, recently closed one of their *maquiladora* facilities in Mexico and moved their data-processing information work to California's San Quentin State Prison because *it saved them money!* So companies like MPS, Inc., will actually bring jobs, once lost to NAFTA, back to the U.S.!

• • •

For a complete look at our prospectus and business plan, write to Mike's Penal Systems, Inc., PO Box 831, Radio City Station, New York, New York 10101.

Mandate?
What Mandate?

REMEMBER THE MORNING of November 9, 1994? We rolled out of bed to headlines proclaiming a REPUBLICAN LANDSLIDE!

"Ohhhhh, where's the toilet, I'm going to be sick."

NEWT GINGRICH . . . SPEAKER OF THE HOUSE!

"Dammit! Where's the Mylanta!"

CHAPTER 19

FOR THE FIRST TIME SINCE 1954, REPUBLICANS CONTROL BOTH HOUSES OF CONGRESS!

"I'm going back to bed. Wake me when the Christian Coalition comes for my fetus."

We all felt just horrible, didn't we? Our country was going to be dismantled by these wide-eyed zealots. And, as if the pounding in our heads wasn't enough, the insipid media and its pundits wouldn't let up on their drumbeat:

The nation has shifted to the right!

The New Deal and the Great Society are finally over!

Democrats had better run for cover!

We were done, cooked, the party was over. Somebody call a priest.

And then I did a little math. By looking at the actual vote counts in the districts where Newt's drones won, the '94 election turned out to be anything *but* a mandate. The Republicans were able to take over Congress by a total of only 38,838 votes *nationwide*. That's right. In a country of 260 million, the Republicans were suddenly governing thanks to the whim of fewer than 39,000 people.

Or, to put it another way, if just 19,500 people had switched their votes in the 13 closest House races, the Democrats would still be in charge and Newt Gingrich would not be Speaker of the House today.

From California to New Jersey, look at the difference just a few votes made in creating this so-called "Republican mandate":

CONGRESSIONAL DISTRICT	REPUBLICAN WINNER	MARGIN OF VICTORY (BY NUMBER OF VOTES)
CA-22	SEASTRAND	1,563
CA-49	BILBRAY	4,686
GA-07	BARR	5,287
KY-01	WHITFIELD	2,502
NE-02	CHRISTENSEN	1,766
NV-01	ENSIGN	1,436
NJ-08	MARTINI	1,833
NC-04	HEINEMAN	1,215
OH-06	CREMEANS	3,422
PA-21	ENGLISH	4,643
WA-05	NETHERCUTT	3,983
WA-09	TATE	5,382
WI-01	NEUMANN	1,120

How big a number is 19,500? About what it takes to fill the Tampa Ice Palace. Or look at it this way: There are nearly fifteen thousand school districts in the United States. If the '94 voters had been spread out across the entire country, that would amount to about <u>one vote per school district</u>. One vote! That could have been you or your aunt or your drinking buddy or the guy who just sold you a Big Gulp at the 7-Eleven. Just one of you and—bam!—Newt would have been toast.

As I've pointed out, over 60 percent of the voting-age population in this country *did not vote* in the 1994 election. Of the remaining 38 percent who did show up at the polls, the Republicans got a little more than half of the vote. That means that Newt Gingrich has been ruling America with only 20 percent of this country having voted for his agenda. Twenty percent! That's no mandate—IT'S A CULT! That's all—just a puny little cult. Nearly 80 percent of all Americans *did not want Newt Gingrich running the show!*

So why were we so afraid of Newt and his "Contract With America"? Everyone got so scared of Gingrich that they just gave up and accepted that the country had made this drastic turn toward the right. Clinton tripped all over himself to praise many parts of the "Contract." Democrats in Congress cowered before the Speaker and quietly licked their wounds. A record number of them announced they would not seek reelection in 1996. Others just switched parties and became Republicans. It was a retreat that was embarrassing to watch.

You can see why most people don't vote. But what happens once the majority of us "check out"? Back in 1992 there was a seat in the Michigan House of Representatives that was decided by *one* vote—and, thanks to a clerical error, it ended up being declared a tie, forcing the Democrats to share power in the House with the Republicans, who had not been in charge since 1969. So you could say that just one person brought on the entire mean-spirited Engler Revolution in Michigan. Because of that one voter, the poor who received general assistance have had their aid entirely eliminated. One single voter caused that to happen.

In 1995, a seat on the Washington, D.C., City Council was also decided by one vote. In Connecticut in 1994, Representative Sam Gejdenson won his seat by only 21 votes. In Alaska that year, Tony Knowles became governor by only 536 votes. That's about three people per Alaskan town.

History is full of singular individuals who, on their own, made a huge difference. If you remember, Jesus had just twelve guys in robes, and Marx only had some old fart named Engels to talk to. Look at how they changed the entire world, for better or worse. It doesn't take Spartacus's army to get something done (in fact, Spartacus lost).

I decided to try an experiment. I asked my research assistant Gillian and my niece Kelsey to randomly call residents of those congressional districts where the Republicans won by just a few votes.

After just a few hours of calling, they were able to persuade six voters who had voted Republican in 1994 to switch their votes to the Democrats in 1996. They are:

Mike Seymore of Spokane

Eric Sonner of Spokane

Lawrence Stephenson of San Diego

Brent Fayer of San Diego

Carl Sain of San Diego

Lillian Caster of Erie

They also got another four people who said they didn't vote in 1994 but will in '96—and they'll vote for the Democrat.

If an overworked book assistant and a twelve-year-old can do this in a matter of three hours, why can't the Democratic National Committee get off its ass and make sure the debacle of '94 isn't repeated?

But that's asking a lot from a party trying desperately to find the middle of the road and sound as Republican as they can.

Hillary, my love

My Forbidden Love for Hillary

CHAPTER 20

I CAN'T REMEMBER when I first fell in love with Hillary Clinton. Maybe it was when I heard her name—it wasn't Clinton! *Rodham,* Hillary *Rodham.* She had kept her name. A politician's wife had kept her own name. I had never heard of such a thing. She also had her own career, made more money than her husband, and spoke out forcefully about children's and women's rights. Back in

1992, I didn't know much about her husband, but I knew I wanted to vote for *her*.

Unfortunately, that was not the choice given to us. So we had to settle for Bill. The world wasn't yet ready for a Hillary.

I don't care about some stupid Arkansas vacation-house deal called Whitewater, or about unloading some White House travel agents or how many changes of hairdo she has had. Hillary Clinton wanted to spend her time making sure we have access to decent health care. But what did we get? A bunch of men whining about how she ran the health care meetings. Big deal. I think for them her only problem was that she was the proud owner of two ovaries.

Here is a woman who has raised a bright, sweet girl in extremely abnormal circumstances. White House aides have repeatedly tried to get Hillary to let them use Chelsea in situations that would enhance the Clinton "family image" with the voters. She has consistently refused to let this happen. That is why, until March of 1996 (when Hillary took Chelsea to Bosnia and they sang Phil Ochs protest songs to the troops), you saw little of Chelsea in public. Why couldn't we have been as blessed with the absence of those Reagan and Bush kids?

With the twisted way the media has dealt with Hillary, we have not been given an accurate portrait of the woman. I think it's because she's smarter than most of the men she encounters, and when that's the case, the woman who's showing off all the brains might as well write her own ticket out of town.

Hillary operates from a moral place in her heart, a really foreign concept in Washington. She is also a deeply religious woman who doesn't wear it on her sleeve but instead lives her life according to her beliefs. How's that, after twelve years of phony Moral Majority posturing with Reagan and Bush while they went about their immoral actions (Iran/Contra, Savings and Loan, etc.)? I always got a kick out of how Ronald Reagan snookered those Bible Belters into backing him—and he hardly ever went to church during his entire eight years in office. Hillary and Bill go every Sunday, holding hands and actually seeming to care about living a moral life.

When it was disclosed during the '92 campaign that Bill might have had a number of affairs, I felt horrible having to watch Hillary baking those chocolate-chip cookies to prove she was a "real woman." To tell you the truth, I didn't want my daughter, Natalie, to see this. I never want her to bake a single chocolate-chip cookie to placate all those sexist assholes out there. Hillary's Betty Crocker impersonation was a humiliation I hope Natalie never has to experience, and I hope, too, that five or ten years from now, the next "Hillary" will not have to bake anything but the dead brain matter of whatever jerk dares to suggest she is anything but an equal.

In the face of these extramarital revelations, Hillary, incredibly, stood by Bill. She went on "60 Minutes" with him and saved his campaign. She said it was enough for her that they had worked it out by themselves, and it was nobody else's damn business. *Everyone* has problems within their marriage and, if anything, the Clintons actually set an example of how, even in the worst of situations, things can be worked out. They had found their way, whatever that way was.

Instead of respecting that—and applauding how they kept their family *together* in the face of adversity—conservatives went on a Hillary Rampage and have never let up. Oh, they love family values, this bunch—the divorced Bob Dole, the divorced Newt Gingrich, the divorced Phil Gramm, the divorced Dick Armey, the divorced Ronald Reagan, the divorced John Engler, and the divorced (twice) Rush Limbaugh. It's not that there's anything wrong with divorce (for the women married to guys like these, it's a moral imperative). I think the American public is finally catching on to this group's two-faced crap.

I have had to spend the past four years in this country listening to my gendermates berate, belittle, and degrade this woman. Whether it is the editors of *Time* and *Newsweek* who continue to run cover photos of her in the most unflattering lighting, or the pundits who run her into the ground whenever the opportunity arises, I wonder if there is anyone willing to break from this testosterone-challenged pack and courageously proclaim: "WE HAVE NEVER SEEN A WOMAN LIKE THIS IN THE WHITE HOUSE AND, MAN, IS SHE EASY ON THE EYES!"

I have to say, while watching the Clintons on "60 Minutes" in 1992, I kept looking at Hillary sitting there with her legs crossed, and found myself being drawn to her in some, how shall we say, *unexplainable* way. And then I remember thinking, "To hell with Bill's affairs—I wonder who's had the privilege of going a few rounds with this ball of fire? Yeee-ouch!"

Oh, I can hear the groans now from you guys out there who think I'm nuts for finding Hillary attractive. Well, fuck you. Get some glasses. HILLARY RODHAM IS ONE HOT SHITKICKIN' FEMINIST BABE.

(In the interests of full disclosure, I must admit at this point that I am happily and monogamously married to the world's most wonderful, beautiful woman, an artist and a better writer than I. In the interests of supporting strong women everywhere, she has indulged me in my forbidden love of Hillary.)

Why do I appear to be alone in this attraction? Why is it that when you search "Hillary Clinton" on the Internet, this is the kind of asinine stuff you get:

Did you hear about Kentucky Fried Chicken's Hillary Combo meal? Two small breasts, two large thighs, and two left wings.

(Note to guys like me: Isn't that a description of nirvana?)

It is doubly distressing to see other women go after Hillary. Instead of praising her for the ground she's broken, they revel in cutting her to shreds. Take, for instance, Maureen Dowd of *The New York Times*. She is fixated on trashing Hillary Clinton in the way liberals love to do, to prove they're not *really* liberal. Check out one of the many snide things Dowd has written about Hillary:

> *Mrs. Clinton's acknowledgments page [in her book* It Takes a Village*] is, in fact, the perfect illustration of her problem. It must be the only acknowledgments page in existence that thanks nobody in particular.*

Or how about this love note from Ms. Dowd regarding Hillary's wardrobe:

> *This rummaging around in the clothes trunk only seems jarring because, by the time people reach Mrs. Clinton's age and position, they have usually found out what works for them and what doesn't.*

I wonder if Dowd could stand the same scrutiny about what "works for" her and how she chooses to give "acknowledgments"? In 1988, I wrote an article for a media watchdog publication in which I revealed how Dowd had allegedly plagiarized a story from the *Congressional Quarterly*, publishing it under her byline in *The New York Times*, an offense that the *Times* kept silent about and that no newspaper other than the *Village Voice* would report on. (It is the unwritten code of the media never to report on your own unless absolutely forced to.) The irony of this is that, at the time, Dowd was reporting on Senator Joe Biden's presidential bid and the charge that he had committed plagiarism in college. Ms. Dowd was reportedly reprimanded internally by her superiors at the *Times,* but later was given a prized column spot on the op-ed page once occupied by the far superior Anna Quindlen.

Maureen didn't seem to like the spotlight being put on *her* when I presented the evidence I had compiled. She told me that this was "a bunch of bullshit" and nothing but "slime being spread by the Biden people." She then hung up on me.

The most vile assaults against Hillary have, in fact, come from *The New York Times* (yes, that *liberal* paper again). Columnist and former Nixon speechwriter William Safire has been in the grip of an enormous Hillary fixation. In his most infamous column about Hillary—which finally brought husband Bill out from under the table to challenge the Nixon hack to fisticuffs—Safire called Hillary a "congenital liar." Congenital means you have the affliction from birth and there's nothing you can do about it. So the man who helped Nixon lie and connive his way through six disgraceful years in the White House calls Hillary Rodham a "congenital liar"? What gall! Safire helped to destroy this country. We have yet to recover from Nixon's Vietnam and Nixon's Watergate. In a more just world, weasels like Safire would be spreading manure on a collective farm somewhere in North Dakota.

But Safire isn't the only one on the Holy Hillary Crusade. Al D'Amato has become the full-time Hillary Senator. While the rest of Congress spent their days trying to run the country, Senator Al was seated in a room by himself, holding his anti-Hillary hearings. They were the most incoherent hearings the Senate has ever seen. Because no one could understand a word he was saying, everyone stopped attending them.

Check out this statistic:

Senate Watergate Hearings: 16 months, 37 witnesses

Senate Whitewater Hearings: 22 months, 159 witnesses

The Whitewater Hearings dragged on so long that D'Amato probably didn't have time to file for divorce (from a wife whom he hasn't lived with in fifteen years) before he went on TV to announce his intentions to marry his *second* wife, Claudia Cohen. But apparently even she got sick of him refusing to leave his Whitewater Hearings room, so she, too, dumped the guy. So, by my count, Al's lost two women because of his obsession with this *one* woman named Hillary. Wow, what a waste of good Italian loving.

Talk radio has also made Hillary its favorite target, bashing her up one side and down the other for a list of sins that, if they weren't filled with so much inciteful violence against her, would be hysterical. Callers like to describe what they would do to her if given the chance.

What does Hillary Clinton do every morning after she shaves her pussy? She sends him off to work in the White House.

Why has Hillary Clinton banned miniskirts in the White House? Because she doesn't want anyone to see her balls.

I have a theory about this growing cottage industry of venom toward Hillary. I think these Hillary Haters have their underwear all in a bunch because it appears THE CLINTONS LIKE TO HAVE SEX! Bill is the first President to come out of the sixties, so you know that means he and Hillary had a *lot* of sex. A thought like that drives a guy like William Safire crazy. He is wound so tight over these two because he missed out on all the fun. Okay, Mr. Safire, so you didn't get any. But can you lighten up a little? Or does it just drive the artery in your neck into a harder knot knowing that this couple, while the Kinks were blasting away on the hi-fi and the buzz from the brownies was reaching its peak, did it in every place imaginable? What's that heavy breathing I hear? Ooooh, Mr. Safire! You're getting a little too red! Shall we call 911?

If we must, let us pity the poor, frightened little men with their trembling penises, struggling to feel an inch better by putting Hillary in her place. What must it be like to have a problem with your dick? I'm not talking about those like me with a legitimate medical excuse. I'm talking about all those poor bastards—the William Bennetts, the John McLaughlins, the Rush Limbaughs—who immediately go limp at the thought of a strong woman. Does the image of the Strong Woman—of "The Hillary" herself!—just pop into their heads without warning, ruining the Big Moment, and causing that special somebody in bed with them to cry, "TIM-BERRRRRR!" as she crawls out from underneath their slimy Republican carcass?

Oh, the sound of falling wood in a Republican forest! Hang in there, Hillary. You'll save the country yet.

A Sperm's Right to Life

I SUPPORT RIGHT TO LIFE. But not for the fetus. That is *not* where life begins. I believe that life begins with the *sperm*. And, as a man, I can tell you from firsthand observation that *billions and billions of sperm are being senselessly slaughtered each and every day!*

You see, I think the Right to Life movement has got it all wrong. They have spent the past twenty-five years defending the rights of "the unborn." Ever since the Supreme Court made abortion legal, the Right to Lifers have been on a mission to reverse that decision. They believe that life begins at conception and that aborting a fetus is the killing of a human life.

Wrong! Wrong! Wrong! Our life does not begin with the fetus. It begins with the *sperm*.

CHAPTER 21

The sperm is the very first building block of life. Without the sperm, there can be no fetus. The fetus is only the "middleman." The sperm is the *kickoff*, not the twenty-yard line.

Yes, I know about the egg. The egg is life, also, and just as important as the sperm. Well, almost as important. While both the sperm and the egg contain an equal number of chromosomes, it is the *sperm* that determines the gender, thus giving it one more job than the egg. Also, the egg has no real work to do except sit there and wait. Nations can fall and whole galaxies can be destroyed, but that egg isn't going anywhere until it's damn good and ready.

The sperm, on the other hand, must compete with at least 200 million other sperm in each ejaculation. They are, in essence, shot out of a cannon, and must literally swim for their survival. Only after a torturous journey through the vagina, the cervix, the uterus and the fallopian tubes do they even stand an infinitesimal chance of fertilizing that egg. Imagine swimming nonstop from Chicago to Detroit during a winter squall. Something like that.

The sperm's head is densely packed with a ton of genetic information. He puts the best computer chip to shame. His midsection, like our bodies, contains the life processes that allow him to stay alive, to move, to do his work. His tail is the appendage that gives him the mobility to travel, much as our legs do for us.

There is no getting around it—the sperm is life. It is not a cell, or a germ, or a microbe. It is the beginning of human life. Without it, none of us would be here. So precious. So sacred.

Yet, each day, all across the globe, men are recklessly aborting their sperm!

What is being done about this?!

Where is the Right to Life movement when they are needed the most? Can't they hear the silent screams of these little babies as their fathers mindlessly dispose of them in a

Kleenex and toss them into the trash? The horror!

Masturbators/killers are snubbing out God-given life. The sperm is not *potential* human life—it *is* human life.

Some of you pro-choice fanatics will point out that the sperm, like the fetus, cannot survive on its own outside the man's body. So what? Life is life! We must stop the premeditated murder committed by men who decide that, for a few moments of pleasure, others must be denied life. Shame! Shame! Shame!

I believe that the Right to Life movement must take up this cause to Save the Sperm. I will personally write to my congressman and insist he support a constitutional amendment making sperm abortion illegal. I will organize pickets outside of buildings where this evil act takes place. Our first stop—fraternity houses. The greatest loss of life, I would think, occurs when "Melrose Place" or "Baywatch" is on. That would be the best time to demonstrate. Then it's off to the YMCA, Boys Town, Rob Lowe's house, all prisons, seminaries, and Motel 6's.

I have already enlisted my staff in this cause. The first thing we decided to do was call the national headquarters of Right to Life to see if they would expand their protests to include this heinous act. We spoke with Christian Polking in the communications department of the National Right to Life Committee. We began by asking him what his views were regarding the sperm being the true beginning of human life. He replied:

> Aristotle and other Greek philosophers believed that life resided in man and that woman was an incubator for the life that sprung from sperm. There are biblical stories [stretching] back into [the] Old Testament . . .
>
> This is not an irrational belief. There needs to be respect for that potentiality [of life in the sperm], but I would draw the line saying that each sperm is a life. . . . [But] it's [not] merely another chemical substance.

It's much more than that. Not something we should toy with . . . [i]t does have a life span of seventy-two hours.

So if it has a life span, it does have a life . . .
It does have a life, but I would draw the line at "human" life. I would not be willing to say that it is human.

Does the egg have a life span?
Yes . . . it travels down the uterus . . . until it is expelled from the body or implanted. . . . An egg and sperm sacrifice their individuality at the moment of fertilization.

If women went around and killed all their eggs with tube-tying and IUDs and medieval torture so they can go out and have sex promiscuously, and men go out and waste their sperm on other men, and other ways—it's hard for me to talk about this—don't you think that is something that the National Right to Life Committee should take up?
Personally, I agree that it is wrong, but I would not want to see the committee doing that because we are single-issue, dealing specifically with abortion, euthanasia, and infanticide . . .
    If we take it to sexual issues, we are fighting a sexual rights battle. . . . People try to make it sound like the Right to Life movement is just a bunch of men out there just trying to oppress women.

That's the most ridiculous thing I've ever heard of.
Yeah, exactly. . . . A right to life is one of our basic rights. . . .

It all comes down to the basics—there are people that would kill

*their own children, because they think they have the right to . . .
the same people who would kill their own sperm and think they
have the right to do that.*

It goes by stages. . . . It's a slippery slope.

*Now, just honestly, have you ever heard my opinion being
expressed—because I want to know that I'm not alone?*

I have heard this before.

Where?

I have spoken to people who have felt the same way, I
have friends who feel the same way.

*There could be a movement. Ten years ago, people weren't even
protesting abortion clinics. . . . If we understood men give life,
we'd be a lot better off.*

It's not just a woman's body we're talking about. . . .
The man plays an instrumental role.

*Instrumental! . . . I just feel better knowing there are people out
there who feel the same way.*

Sure, there are.

• • •

I have the feeling that one day these Right to Lifers will wise
up and expand their mission to include my concerns. Until
then . . .

Can somebody hand me a Kleenex?

DEATH TO WOMEN WHO ABORT!

Dozens of Right to Life members of Congress want a constitutional amendment declaring that life begins at conception and that a fetus is a human being. Most of them used to be against abortion in *all* cases, no exceptions. Then they modified this to all cases *except* when the life of the mother is in danger. Others, though, changed their minds and now feel that a fetus is human life *except* when the life of the mother is in danger *and except* when she has been raped *and except* when she is the victim of incest.

I can't keep up with all the exceptions. As I've said, life is life. Once we all decide on the starting point, that's it. If it becomes part of our Constitution that the fetus is a human life, we must be consistent and treat that *life* the same as all other, more fully developed humans. We cannot have two sets of standards—one for the fetus and one for the rest of us. We should have the same set of rules for everybody in America, right?

With that in mind, I have a few proposals I'd like to offer should this "Human Life" amendment pass:

1. Everyone's age will be calculated from the day of *conception.* If we are "human" from the moment of conception, then the day conception happens—that's our birthday! No longer will we start counting our age from when we leave the womb. After the constitutional amendment becomes law, we will refer to *that* day as our "Womb Liberation Day." I hope Right to Life will push for legislation that marks our *birth* day as the day the sperm fertilizes the egg, which makes us, according to them, a "human being." And each of us will automatically add nine months onto all of our current ages. So, if you're now just four months past your 42d birthday, order the party favors—'cause you're already 43!!

2. Social Security numbers should immediately be assigned to all fetuses. That goes without saying.

3. Capital punishment for all women who have abortions. Right to Life must be consistent; if they truly believe the fetus is a human life, then they must demand the same punishment you or I would get if we were to gun down a guy in the street. A life is a life. To let the "murderous" mother go scot-free would be a travesty. Give her what we gave Ted Bundy! A murderer is a murderer. Right to Life has spent years getting the whole country all gooey-eyed by showing us those pictures of the little fetuses with their little heartbeats and their tiny little hands and feet. "Look, they're *human!*" If they're human, then we must prosecute the mother who slaughters this little innocent. Thirty-eight states now have the death penalty for premeditated murder.

4. The same goes for the doctor who performs the abortion. He's even worse than the mother because he's murdering for profit. So where are the provisions in the Human Life amendment guaranteeing that the doctor is punished? Fry the physicians!

If the Right to Lifers are not willing to adopt the above positions, then is it possible, just possible, they don't *really* believe life begins at conception and that the fetus is *not* a human being? Could it be that this whole anti-abortion movement is actually not about "abortion" at all—but rather about controlling women and their bodies and keeping them "in their place"?

Just asking.

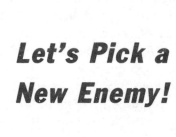

Let's Pick a
New Enemy!

GORBACHEV, THAT WANKER. Before he came
along, we had a great little scam going.
From 1946 to 1988, our American leaders pounded into us that the Soviet
Union was the Evil Empire, a huge Red
Menace that would brainwash our youth
and that, worst of all, had the capacity to
blow us to smithereens. This was, on its
face, true. But the Soviet
Union never developed
the technology for any
nuclear weapons system first; we would
always initiate the latest, greatest missile and then they would have to play
catch-up. The Soviets, unlike us, never
sent a half million ground troops
10,000 miles from home to invade
countries and fight wars; they confined
their military suppression to countries
that bordered theirs (just because they
were a little freaked out after being

invaded for centuries and then lost 25 million people in World War II was no reason for them to be concerned, right?). And the Soviets never dropped the Bomb—that distinction, to this day, belongs solely to us.

Washington, though, never let up on reminding us of the grave peril we were in—and most of us fell for it. We lived our lives under this weird shadow of terror that the world could end at any moment. But this manufactured fear had a huge upside: it kept our economy humming along, making record profits for the defense industry and employing millions of Americans. The threat of thermonuclear holocaust was indeed good for business.

The other positive side effect of the Cold War for our elected officials was that it gave them a way to distract us from what was going on at home. As long as they could keep us worried more about the *external* threats, we didn't pay much attention to the fact that our cities were crumbling, that our schools sucked, and that the number of jobs available was being permanently downsized.

Then one day, Mikhail Gorbachev, the Soviet Man-in-Charge, decided to call the whole thing off. He said he didn't want to play with us anymore. He unilaterally stopped building nuclear bombs. He said, "I don't care what you do in the U.S., I'm checking out of this insanity." Then he tore down the Berlin Wall. He told everybody in Eastern Europe he was bringing his troops home and they should elect their own leaders.

What nerve this guy had! The Cold War was a sweet deal for both of our countries. But once it was over, there was no bogeyman for us to fight. We started to look around at home and, man, we were shocked. While we had been spending billions on a useless arms race, our roads, sewer systems, and everything else were collapsing around us. Suddenly we looked up and saw some homeless guy begging us for a quarter. Then another homeless guy a block away.

Then two homeless guys—jeez, how did this happen? Before we knew it, we were all working in shitty, low-paying jobs—those of us who had jobs. Millions of people who used to build the nuclear submarines, process the plutonium, design the Stealth fighters, and service the local army base, were now out of work because they were not building things that consumers buy. While we spent 50 percent of our tax dollars fighting commies, the Japanese spent 1 percent of their GNP on their military and concentrated on the needs of their people.

With no Cold War to fight, America has been adrift lately, unable to find a focus for our existence. Ending up "the winner" and holding the title as the World's Only Superpower is not as exciting as we always thought it would be. It's kind of hard to feel like a superpower when you don't have any competition. If there is no way to show your prowess against an enemy, then what makes you so "super"? Does only one team go to the Super Bowl? What if every year just the Dallas Cowboys were allowed to go to the Big Game? What would they do with themselves? Run around in a circle at the fifty-yard line shouting, "We're the Super Team! We're number one! Nyah, nyah, nyah-nyah-nyah!"

Embarrassing.

America just hasn't been the same since we lost a reason to hate. With no enemy from the outside, we seem to have turned on ourselves. Oklahoma City, the militias, Pat Buchanan—how pathetic! Without another country to spew venom against, many Americans have been left to their own means in finding a new enemy—and the results have not been pretty.

So I ask you: WHY HATE OURSELVES WHEN THERE ARE STILL MORE THAN 180 COUNTRIES LEFT TO FIGHT?

The solution is so simple, I can't believe anyone in Washington hasn't thought of it. All we need to do is pick one of the many countries that dot the globe and designate it as the official new Evil Empire. And as soon as we do that, we'll all be back to work!

To help the President and the Joint Chiefs of Staff select our new adversary, I have put together a list of countries that, although not as big and bad as the Soviet Union, will certainly live up to their potential if given half a chance.

The key thing to remember here is that we want a *Cold War* with one of these nations. *Cold* Wars last at least fifty years. Everybody gets a job. And no one is ever killed in an actual battle between the two superpowers. Real wars—like Grenada, Panama, and Iraq—last for only a few hours. That simply isn't long enough to jump-start the economy.

So get out your maps and your little toy soldiers as I take you into Mike's Situation Room, deep under the bowels of Manhattan, to peruse our options. It's time to pick a new enemy!

POSSIBLE CANDIDATES FOR OUR "NEW ENEMY"

Libya. This country has been begging to play the part for some time. Led by the cross-dressing Muammar Khaddafi, Libya meets many of the necessary requirements for Most-Hated Status. We think they may have had something to do with blowing up Pan Am flight 103 (suspicion alone is enough for us to send in the Marines; the proof we can always manufacture later). Libya also keeps trying to make nuclear weapons—and, in a slap to the rest of the world, it refuses to field a team for the Winter Olympics. But it has no problem sending millions of dollars to Louis Farrakhan. *What are we waiting for?*

China. In a perfect world, this should be our best bet—but too many American corporations have set up shop there in the past decade. There is no way Washington is going to harass a country that has become the Sweatshop for America. I remember a few years ago back in Flint, General Motors, in order not to cause an uproar, secretly tore out an entire engine plant and, in the middle of the night, packed up major parts of the assembly line and sent it off to China. GM isn't alone in this move to China; hundreds of American companies are doing business there. So I guess we can kiss the Chinese good-bye as the new enemy. Plus, there's 1.2 billion of them and only 263 million of us. I say leave 'em alone.

Iran. Been there.

Iraq. Done that.

North Korea. I know, I know, we've done them also, and who wants to cover the same ground twice? But these lunatics still haven't got it through their thick heads that the world can't relate to a country whose capital—Pyongyang—cannot be pronounced. If you can't say it, why go there? To make matters worse, ever since their leader for life, Kim Il Sung, died in 1994, they haven't chosen anyone to replace him. Their "meeting" to select a new premier has been going on for nearly two years. Think of the coffee-and-doughnuts bill!

They're afraid to put Kim's son in charge because he watches too many movies. In fact, he owns over 20,000 videotapes and laser disks—considered to be the largest home video collection in the world. It would be hard to engage this enemy when its leader is busy watching *Caddyshack II* for the eighteenth time.

I still think they'd make a worthy enemy: they've got the largest army in the world (per capita), they probably have nuclear weapons, and until this year, they have refused to participate in *either* the Summer or Winter Games.

Cuba. Forget it. Castro already beat us. (See chapter 23, "Those Keystone Cubans.")

Burma. Even American businesses are repulsed by this place and the way they treat their citizens. Thanks to years of terror, summary executions, ethnic genocide, forced labor, and shipping 60 percent of all heroin that comes into the United States, just about everyone except Texaco, Unocal, and Arco has pulled out of this country. In 1988, Burma went and changed its name to the "Union of Myanmar," thinking they could fool us. I say let's give them a Burma Shave. They are ripe for attack by . . . NO! WAIT! We don't want to *attack* anyone! Think: "*Cold* War *Cold* War *Cold* War *Cold* War . . ."

Switzerland. Just once I'd like to see these wimps get involved in a real war so they would know what the rest of us have had to go through. They're famous for always sitting it out. They were also the last European country to give women the right to vote (not until 1971!). I think if we just announced tomorrow that we were going after their yodeling ass, we'd see just how "neutral" they are. I'll bet you the banks in Zurich will be working overtime to buy every available nuclear weapon on the market.

Canada. I think I saw this idea in a movie once.

Burkina Faso. Here's another country that went and changed the name the invading Europeans generously gave them. It used to be called "Upper Volta," which was always good for a laugh in Mrs. LaCombe's fourth-grade geography class. This is probably the second-poorest country on the planet after Bangladesh, but each year they throw the biggest film festival on the African continent. Go figure. There is absolutely no one in America who knows where this country is—and that alone could work in its favor for being really scary:

"I hear *Burkina Faso* is pointing nuclear missiles at New York!"

"Oh my God! Where is Burkina Faso?!"

"NO . . . ONE . . . CAN . . . FIND . . . THEM!"

That is the A-list of possible new Evil Empires. Which is your favorite? Send your vote to me and I'll personally deliver the results to the Pentagon. Postcards only. Send them to: "Mike Picks a New Enemy," P.O. Box 831, Radio City Station, New York, New York 10101. I'll announce the results along with Wolf Blitzer on "The Larry King Show" sometime in the near future.

Those Keystone Cubans

HAVE YOU EVER wondered how Fidel Castro has stayed in power for so long? No one, other than the King of Jordan and the Prince of Monaco, has been in the top spot for a greater period of time. The man has outlasted eight U.S. presidents, ten Olympic Games, and the return of Halley's Comet. And no matter what the United States government does to try to dethrone him, he's got more lives than John Travolta has comebacks.

CHAPTER 23

It's not that our American leaders haven't given it their best effort. Ever since Castro liberated his country from the corrupt U.S.- and Mafia-backed Batista regime, Washington has tried a variety of methods to unseat him. These have included taxpayer-funded assassination attempts, invasions, blockades, embargoes, threats of nuclear annihilation, internal disruption, intimidation, and biological warfare (the CIA dropped a bunch of African Swine Fever germs over the country in 1971, forcing the Cubans to destroy 500,000 pigs).

And, something that has always seemed strange to me, there is an actual U.S. naval base *on the island of Cuba!* Imagine if, after defeating the British in our Revolution, we then let them keep a few thousand troops and a bunch of battleships in New York Harbor. Weird.

President Kennedy, who followed through with President Eisenhower's plan to invade Cuba at the Bay of Pigs, ordered the CIA to kill Castro, trying everything from a pen filled with poisoned ink to an exploding cigar. (No, I do not get my information from Maxwell Smart; it's all in the Church Committee report from the U.S. Congress, 1975.)

Of course, nothing worked. Castro became stronger and the U.S. continued to go nuts. Cuba was seen as "the one that got away." It became an embarrassment to us. Here we had every nation in this hemisphere in our back pocket—except those damn Cubans. It looked bad. Like when the whole family goes out to dinner and the one bad seed, little Billy, just won't sit still and do what he is told. Everyone in the place is looking at the parents and wondering just what kind of job they're doing. The appearance that they have no discipline or control is the worst humiliation. So they start whacking little Billy, but forget about it—he ain't ever going to finish his peas.

That's how silly we look to the rest of the world. Like we've been driven insane over this little island ninety miles from our shores. We don't feel that way about a real threat to humanity, like the one posed by the Chinese government. Talk about a bunch of thugs! Yet we can't move fast enough to hop into bed with them. Washington spent twenty-three years getting us all worked up against the Chinese—and then, suddenly, one day they're our friends.

It turned out that the Republicans and their corporate bud-dies weren't *really* against communist dictators—just those who wouldn't let them come in and make a buck.

And that, of course, has been Castro's fatal mistake. Once he took over and nationalized all the American businesses and booted the Mob out of Havana, he might as well have taken a seat on the San Andreas Fault, because the wrath of Uncle Sam came down on him hard, and it hasn't let up for over thirty-seven years. Yet Castro has survived. For that accomplishment alone, despite all of his flaws (political repression, four-hour speeches, and a literacy rate in Cuba of 100 percent), you gotta admire the guy.

So why do we continue to fight this leftover turkey leg from the Cold War? The answer can be found by looking no further than a town called Miami. It is there that a nutty bunch of Cuban exiles have controlled U.S. foreign policy regarding this insignificant island nation. These Cubans, many of whom were Batista supporters and lived high on the hog while that crook ran the country, seem not to have slept a wink since they grabbed their assets and headed to Florida.

And, since 1960, they have insisted on pulling us into their madness. Why is it that in *every* incident of national torment that has deflated our country for the past three decades—the Kennedy assassination, Watergate, Iran-Contra, our drug abuse epidemic—the list goes on and on—we find that the Cuban exiles are always present and involved? First it was Lee Harvey Oswald's connection to the Cubans in New Orleans. (Or was it the Cuban exiles acting alone to kill Kennedy, or Castro ordering the assassination 'cause he just got bored with Kennedy trying to bump *him* off? Whichever theory you subscribe to, the Cubans are lurking in the neighborhood.)

Then, on the night of June 17, 1972, three Cubans—Bernard Barker, Eugenio Martinez, and Virgilio Gonzalez (plus Americans Frank Sturgis and James McCord Jr.)—were caught breaking into the Watergate offices of the chairman of the Democratic Party. This covert operation eventually brought down Richard Nixon, so I guess there is a silver lining to that particular Cuban-exile operation.

Today, Barker and Gonzalez are considered heroes in Miami's Cuban community. Martinez, later pardoned by Ronald Reagan, is the only one who feels bad. "I did not want myself to be involved in the downfall of the President of the United States." Oh, well, how nice of you!

When Ollie North needed a cover group to run arms into Nicaragua to help overthrow the government, who else could he turn to but the Miami Cubans? Bay of Pigs veterans Ramón Medina and Rafael Quintero were key managers of the air-transport company that supplied weapons to the Contras. The U.S.-backed Contra War was responsible for the deaths of thirty thousand Nicaraguans.

One of the big bonuses to come out of our funding of these Cuban exiles was the help they gave us in bringing illegal drugs into the States, destroying families and whole sections of our cities. Beginning in the early sixties, a number of Cubans (who also participated in the Bay of Pigs invasion) began running major narcotics rings in this country. The DEA found little support within the federal government to go after these Cuban exiles, because they had organized themselves under the phony banner of "freedom groups." In fact, most were nothing more than fronts for massive drug-smuggling operations. These same drug runners later helped to run arms to the Contras.

U.S.-based Cuban terrorist organizations have been responsible for more than two hundred bombings and at least a hundred murders since Castro's revolution. They have got everyone so afraid to stand up to them that I probably shouldn't even be writing this chapter. I am, after all, one of the few unarmed Americans.

So why am I not worried? Because these Cuban exiles, for all their chest-thumping and terrorism, are really just a bunch of wimps. That's right. Wimps.

Need proof? For starters, when you don't like the oppressor in your country, you stay there and try to overthrow him. This can be done by force (American Revolution, French Revolution) or through peaceful means (Gandhi in India or Mandela in South Africa). But you don't just turn tail and run like these Cubans.

Imagine if the American colonists had all run to Canada—and then insisted the Canadians had a *responsibility* to overthrow the British down in the States. The Sandinistas never would have freed their country from Somoza if they had all been sitting on the beach in Costa Rica, drinking margaritas and getting rich. Mandela went to prison, not to Libya or London.

But the wealthy Cubans scooted off to Miami—and got wealthier. Ninety percent of these exiles are white, while the majority of Cubans—62 percent—are black or of mixed race. The whites knew they couldn't stay in Cuba because they had no support from the people. So they came here, expecting us to fight their fight for them. And, like morons, we have.

It's not that these Cuban crybabies haven't tried to help themselves. But a quick look at their efforts resembles an old Keystone Kops movie. The Bay of Pigs is their best-known fiasco. It had all the elements of a great farce—wrong boats, wrong beach, no ammo for the guns, no one shows up to meet them, and, finally, they are left for dead, wandering around a part of their island completely unfamiliar to them (their limo drivers, I guess, had never taken them there in the good old days).

This embarrassment was so monumental the world still hasn't stopped laughing—and the Miami Cubans have never forgotten or forgiven this. Say "Bay of Pigs" to any of them, and you might as well be a dentist with a drill on a raw, decaying nerve.

You would think that the Bay of Pigs defeat would have taught them a lesson, but then you would probably be projecting. You would have given up. Not this crowd. Since 1962, numerous Cuban exile groups have attempted even more raids to "liberate" their homeland.

Let's go to the highlights reel:

• In 1981, a group of Miami Cuban exiles landed on Providenciales Island in the Caribbean on their way to invading Cuba. Their boat, the only one of four exile boats to make it out of the Miami River (the other three were turned back by the Coast Guard due to foul weather, engine trouble, or too few life jackets), ran aground on a reef near Providenciales. Stuck there on the island with no food or shelter, the Miami Cubans started fighting among themselves. They begged the people of Miami to rescue them off the island, and after three weeks they were airlifted back to Florida. The only one of their group to make it to Cuban waters, Geraldo Fuentes, suffered an appendicitis attack while at sea and had to be helicoptered by the Coast Guard to Guantanamo for treatment.

• In 1968, a group of Miami Cubans learned that a Polish ship was docked in the port of Miami and that a Cuban delegation might be aboard the freighter. From the MacArthur Causeway, according to the St. Petersburg Times, the Cuban exiles fired a homemade bazooka and hit the ship's hull. It only put a nick in the ship, and the group's leader, Orlando Bosch, was sentenced to ten years in prison, but was released in 1972. Bosch explained that they had hoped to cause more damage, but, he pleaded, "It was a *big* ship!" Bosch had earlier been arrested for towing a torpedo through downtown Miami during rush hour, and another time he was caught with six hundred aerial bombs loaded with dynamite in the trunk of his Cadillac. In 1990, the Bush administration released him from prison, where he was serving time for parole violations.

• According to *Washington Monthly*, "During the summer and early fall of 1963, five commando raids were launched against Cuba in the hopes of destabilizing the regime. The negligible Cuban underground was instructed to leave faucets running and lightbulbs burning to waste energy."

• In 1962, according to the *San Francisco Chronicle*, Cuban exile José Basulto, on a CIA-sponsored mission, fired a 20-mm cannon from a speedboat at the Incan Hotel next to Havana Bay, hoping to kill Fidel Castro. The shell missed, and Basulto, seeing gasoline spilling all over his boat, high-tailed it back to Florida. "One of our gas tanks, made of plastic, began to leak," Basulto explained later. "Gas ran all over the deck. We didn't know what to do."

Years later, Basulto would go on to form "Brothers to the Rescue," an exile group that for the past few years has been flying missions over Cuba, buzzing Cuban sites, dropping leaflets, and generally trying to intimidate the Cuban government. In February 1996, Castro was apparently fed up with this harassment, and after the twenty-fifth incident in the past twenty months of the Brothers violating Cuban airspace, he ordered that two of their planes be shot down.

Even though Brothers to the Rescue was violating U.S. law by flying into Cuban airspace (a fact the FAA acknowledges), the Clinton administration again went to the exile trough and instantly got a bill passed to tighten the embargo against Cuba. This embargo has brought the wrath of the rest of the world against us—the UN General Assembly voted 117 to 3 to "condemn" the United States for its economic violence against Cuba (as it has in every vote since the embargo was imposed).

The week after the planes were shot down, the exiles tried to force the hand of the U.S., hoping to get the military to engage in some kind of action against Castro. They announced that on the following Saturday they would take a flotilla of boats from Florida to just off the Cuban coast, to protest the loss of the two planes. Clinton decided to stage the greatest show of force against Cuba since the Missile Crisis, and sent a squadron of F-15 fighters, eleven Coast Guard cutters, two Navy missile cruisers, one Navy frigate, two C-130 planes, and a bevy of choppers, AWACs, and six hundred coast guardsmen to support the flotilla.

All he forgot to send was the Dramamine—which, it turned out, was what the Miami Cubans really needed. Just forty miles out of Key West, the Cubans on the boats started getting seasick, heaving up big chunks and begging their skippers to turn the damn yachts around. With the whole world watching, the Cubans once again turned tail and ran. When they got back to port, they held a press conference to explain their retreat. One spokesman was still a little woozy, and you could see the journalists backing away from him, expecting any moment to be covered with a Linda Blair Special.

"A horrible storm arose out on the sea," said the rapidly paling Cuban exile leader. "The waves were over ten feet high, and we had to turn back or lose our ships!" As he spoke, some creative genius working the weekend shift at CNN ran footage of the flotilla taken from the air as it headed toward Cuba. The sun was shining, the sea was as smooth as glass, and the wind blew gently, if at all. Reporters out at sea did say that after the CNN cameras left, the waters became "rather rough." I'm sure they did.

Castro had to be laughing his ass off.

What America Needs
Is a Makeover

EVER SINCE I can remember, the United States has not been a very popular country. Take a poll, from Zimbabwe to Uruguay, and for some unexplained reason, you'll find that other people just hate our guts.

My first memory of our not winning any popularity contests is of seeing some angry Venezuelans hurling a grapefruit at Richard Nixon's limo on TV. From that point on, it's just been a steady stream of flag burnings,

embassy takeovers, hostage nabbings, effigy hangings, terrorist bombings, random hijackings, and, once these foreigners got smart, the nationalization of all KFC outlets.

Why the bum's rush? They love our movies, our music, our blue jeans. Okay, so we're a little arrogant and pushy with that "We're Number One" stuff. But if you had to live in a country with Chuck Norris, you'd probably act the same way, too.

And I can understand why they don't like us sending troops to invade their countries. But talk about holding a grudge! Just because we killed two million Vietnamese and never gave them a dime in the reparations we promised them is no reason to believe we'll get that carried away again. Sure, we've sent in the Marines to nine other countries *since* Vietnam, but that should *not* be cause for alarm.

We are not a perfect nation. We've made our mistakes. And now we have an image problem. We are hated, despised, reviled, cursed, and spat upon the world over.

I think it's time for that to change. I think it's time we had a makeover.

These days, lots of companies are finding that a "new look" helps improve their image with the public. After it was discovered that Hooker Chemical Company had contaminated the Love Canal area of Niagara Falls, they looked really bad in the media. No problem. They just sold the company and changed their name to Occidental. Like *accidental,* but with an *o.* See, they have a sense of humor.

After some crazy guy spiked a bunch of Tylenol bottles with poison, killing seven people, Tylenol responded immediately, opening a telephone hot line to answer consumer concerns. They developed a plastic protective seal that became the standard in the drug industry. It was considered one of the greatest public relations turnarounds ever.

Well, that's exactly what America needs right now. And instead of spending millions hiring a public relations firm to design the campaign, I hereby offer my services, free of charge. The President has my permission to use any or all of the following ideas to create a better-looking, smoother-tasting, go-down-easy America:

A NEW NAME

"The United States of America"? Long. Boring. Ugh. Sounds to me like the Founding Fathers got tired of arguing over what to call the new country ("Hey, I like 'Columbia.'" "How about 'The New, Improved New England'?" "Let's just call it 'George and Martha's Place'"). So they gave up and settled for a very pedestrian name, actually more like a description. There were "states," and they were "united." "United States." Brilliant.

It's too bad they left this item until last on the agenda back in 1776. They spent an inordinate amount of time on minor matters like the Declaration of Independence and the Articles of Confederation. Nobody today remembers what those documents say, but *everybody* remembers the name of the country.

The British didn't do it that way when they got their start. They decided to call themselves "Great Britain"—and look where that positive, upbeat attitude got them, considering there's really nothing "great" about the British. But they knew a name like that would make other countries tremble in fear ("Ooooh, they're just too *great* to mess with!") and it worked for hundreds of years. Native peoples of foreign lands, seeing a British battleship offshore, knew they were in trouble: "What's that say on the side of the ship?" "It says . . . 'GREAT'!" "Oh my God! Raise the white flag!" They never would have got that far if they had called themselves "Combined Districts on an Island." And when they later changed it to "United Kingdom," they knew enough to follow up the word *United* with the word *Kingdom*. Not *States*. *Kingdom* sounds like they're going to kick your ass.

Besides, as soon as we came up with "The United States of America," people realized it was too long and just started shortening us to "America." We weren't called "United Statesters"; we were known as "Americans." But that little trick didn't get us moved up to the front of the list of nations—we're still stuck in the *U*'s near the end of any roll call.

We need a new name for a new century! Here are my suggestions:

The Big One. Short, to the point. "Where you from?" "I'M FROM THE BIG ONE!" Nobody messes with you then.

Atlantic & Pacific, or *"A&P."* Quaint, and helpful to those looking for our location between the two oceans on the map. It also reminds one of food—always a plus.

Land o' Sex. Sex sells. Will make everyone sorry they don't live here. Could cause even greater influx of illegal aliens.

Ebony and Ivory. They say we are "a house divided" by race. This name will help to bring us together.

USAWorld. America as theme park. Who doesn't love a theme park? Rides instead of crime! Clowns instead of elected leaders! Tokens instead of taxes! It's a winner any way you look at it.

Americapalooza. Baby boomers won't understand this one, but they'll be dead soon anyway.

Planet USA. Not a restaurant, a nation, but it lets enemies know that they have to deal with Arnold, Sly, and Bruce if they try any funny business.

Hard Rock America. Backup plan if we can't get the rights to use "Planet USA" from Arnold, Sly, and Bruce.

A NEW FLAG

The current flag is not a popular icon around the globe. It's like waving a red cape at a mad bull. People see those Stars and Stripes and for some reason they just go insane. Why give them this all-too-easy symbol on which they can vent their rage?

I have a few ideas for a new design. I am not a very good artist—certainly no Betsy Ross!—but here are a few rough ideas I'd like to propose of what to put on our new flag:

1. Head of Newt emitting radio beams from his ears. (Now, here's a flag they can burn and feel good about it!)

2. Lots of big, scary guys. (The best defense is a strong offense.)

3. George Washington riding Barney. (Something old, something new.)

4. Praying hands holding a dollar bill. (Says we're a Christian country and we got lots o' loot.)

5. Positions from the Kama Sutra. (Again, sex sells. Hindu images, though, may be confusing.)

A NEW SLOGAN

"In God We Trust" sort of lets us off the hook in taking responsibility for our own actions. Why don't we leave God out of our problems? He probably has enough of his own.
How about one of these snappy new slogans:

"America: In by 10, Out by 2"

"A Really Good Place to Order a Thick, Juicy Steak"

"Checks Cashed Here"

"Our Citizens Are Armed and They Like to Shoot"

"The United States of America! You Got a Better Idea?"

A NEW SYMBOL

Forget about the bald eagle. I've never seen one, and if a member of the animal kingdom is going to represent itself as my national symbol, it better get busy and start procreating. There are hardly any of these damn things left.

My daughter, Natalie, suggests that we replace the bald eagle with the bald man. There's millions of them, so the icon will feel familiar, friendly—and hairless.

A NEW NATIONAL ANTHEM

On this point, I know I have no opposition. Let's dump this unsingable, irrelevant song and replace it with that song they always play at the ball game: "We Will, We Will Rock You."

• • •

If we were to try just a few of my suggestions, I believe our standing in the court of world opinion would be greatly enhanced. If you have any ideas that will help our country out, feel free to pass them on to the White House, 1600 Pennsylvania Avenue NW, Washington, D.C. 20500, or phone (202) 456-1414. I'm sure they're open to just about anything right now.

O.J.
Is Innocent

WHEN YOU'RE WHITE like me, and you believe that O. J. Simpson did not kill Nicole Brown Simpson and Ronald Goldman, life can get very, very lonely. Nearly all of your friends think you've taken a vacation from reality. They caution you not to repeat your belief in his innocence in public, and certainly not in this book.

White people are very upset about the O.J. verdict. *Very* upset. But why? Because a killer was set free? That happens every day. Because O.J. beat his wife? Excuse me, that's going on next door to you. Right now. Have you called the police yet, or do you just not want to "get involved"?

If you are black, you already know the reasons why White America is so angry at the O.J. verdict, and you probably

CHAPTER 25

know what I'm about to say. Feel free to skip ahead to the next chapter.

I have never believed O. J. Simpson, with his own hands, killed these two people. I *do* believe he is one of the biggest pieces of shit walking the planet Earth, but that only puts him in the company of about 10 million other men who abuse women and the other billion or so of us who let them get away with it.

We don't want to acknowledge that, as a society, we let O.J. get away with beating the crap out of Nicole. Only after she was left dead and mutilated on a sidewalk on South Bundy Drive did we get on our high horse and demand justice. Did we want justice, or absolution for our inaction?

All of these questions have led me to wonder if it is possible in America for us to fairly judge an evil man. In other words, if this man O.J. commits nine evil acts (physical beatings, threats, trespassing, forced entry, psychological abuse, destruction of property, stalking, window-peeping, and adultery)—but he does not commit the tenth one (murder)—does he deserve to be found innocent of the one crime he *didn't* commit? Or, because we failed to punish him for the other nine crimes he *was* responsible for, does that give us the right to get out the noose and hang him now . . . because *we* screwed up?

I don't think so. I know most of you believe he did it, and I respect why you may feel that way—it sure appears the son of a bitch was right there that night with all his sick anger and jealousy—but what *if* he wasn't? None of us, including me, knows for sure if he was involved. Only O.J. and Kato the Akita Dog know if he committed this horrible crime. I'd like to walk you through my reasoning as to why O.J. probably didn't do it—and what the larger implications of this case are for those of us who live in this very divided America.

1. Nothing the L.A. Police Say Should Ever Be Believed.
This is one of the most corrupt, dishonest, racist, and violent police forces in the world. Case after case from the LAPD and the L.A. Sheriff's Department during the past decade does nothing but point up what a bunch of thugs many of those who wear that black uniform are. Nothing has amazed me more during the O.J. ordeal than how otherwise intelligent, liberal-minded people have forgotten what the term "L.A. police" means.

Please allow me to remind you of the following:

• In 1993, L.A. police officers killed Michael James Bryant, a popular Pasadena barber, asphyxiating him in the backseat of a police car after hog-tying and beating him. The coroner ruled his death a homicide.

• In June 1992, an unarmed African-American tow-truck driver, John L. Daniels Jr., pulled into a Chevron service station on the corner of Florence and Crenshaw—just two miles from the flashpoint of the April 1992 riots. While pumping gas, he was approached by two white L.A. motorcycle police officers, including Douglas Iversen, a fifteen-year veteran with a history of misconduct. After an argument over his registration, Daniels became exasperated and tried to leave. He was promptly shot dead in his truck by Iversen. Area residents described Daniels's death as a public execution, according to writer Mike Davis in the *Los Angeles Times*. Iversen was not fired until March 1995.

• Between 1988 and 1994, in at least eight cases, female police officers alleged that they were sexually assaulted by men in the LAPD. One police officer allegedly raped two female counterparts while off duty, shoving a 9-millimeter pistol into one woman, ice cubes into the other.

• In 1985, Officer Ronald L. Benegas pleaded guilty to burglary in connection with an LAPD burglary ring involving twelve officers. Benegas, who admitted to committing more than a hundred burglaries while on duty, said that he and another officer would break store windows using marbles fired from slingshots. Then, while ostensibly responding to the alarms, they would steal the merchandise.

• In 1991, a commission headed by now–Secretary of State Warren Christopher confirmed the commonplace use of excessive force and systemic racism throughout the LAPD.

• And, of course, there was the beating of Rodney King, which I don't need to rehash for you on these pages.

I have felt, long before O.J., that anything the L.A. Police Department says must, at first, *not be believed*. For any of us to believe another individual, we have to trust them. Have the L.A. police earned your trust? Because they have violated that trust, I am forced to presume they are lying whenever they speak, and only when they can prove that they are not lying can I believe their version of anything.

I don't understand why so many people have believed the version of events that took place on Bundy that night as laid out by this corrupt department. What miracle did they perform to gain the trust of so many Americans?

The "police version" of Ron's and Nicole's murders was developed, in part, by a detective named Mark Fuhrman. "Oh, if only the prosecution hadn't called Fuhrman!" That's what people like to say. As if Fuhrman was no more than a "tactical error" instead of perhaps the root of what is wrong here. The day the "Fuhrman tapes" were played in Judge Ito's courtroom to determine whether the jury should hear them, I happened to be watching the trial live. The tapes were so damaging to the efforts by the media to convict O.J. in the court of public opinion that no network newscast that night played them verbatim and in full. *The New York Times* did not run a transcript of them the next day. Unless you were watching TV live at eleven-thirty that morning, the *full* text of what Fuhrman said was kept from you. Here are the uncensored highlights from Mark Fuhrman's taped conversations with screenwriter Laura McKinney.

(Keep in mind that the jury never heard *any* of these remarks by Fuhrman.)

MARK FUHRMAN (referring to a suspect): "[I]f I would have arrested the son of a bitch, I would have killed him. If I ever see the son of a bitch and we're alone, I would kill him. . . . [D]ead men tell no tales."

MARK FUHRMAN: "Most real good policemen understand that they would just love to take certain people and just take them to the alley and just blow their brains out."

MARK FUHRMAN: "We stopped the choke because a bunch of niggers have a bunch of those organizations in the South End and because all niggers were choked out and killed— twelve in ten years. Really extraordinary, isn't it?"

MARK FUHRMAN: "Westwood is gone. The niggers have discovered it."

MARK FUHRMAN: "There is going to be a massacre in the future and they know that. There is the Rolling Sixties, a nigger group, they went into a sporting goods store and stole fifty Uzis, 3,000 rounds."

MARK FUHRMAN: "First thing, anything out of a nigger's mouth for the first five or six sentences is a fucking lie. . . . You keep choking him until he tells you the truth. You know, it is kind of funny, but a lot of policemen will get a kick out of it."

MARK FUHRMAN: "We basically got impatient with him being so fucking stupid. . . . So we . . . just went the 'scenic route' to the station. . . . Dana goes, 'No blood, Mark.' 'No problem, not even any marks, Dana.' Just body shots. Did you ever try to find a bruise on a nigger? It's pretty tough, huh?"

MARK FUHRMAN: "[W]hen he gives me his driver's license, I'll just rip the fucker up."

MARK FUHRMAN: "I had sixty-six allegations of brutality. . . . We grabbed a girl that lived there. . . . Grabbed her by her head and used her as a barricade. Walked up and told them, 'I got this girl, I'll blow her fuckin' brains out if you come out with a gun.' Held her like this, threw the bitch down the stairs. . . . I must have three or four thousand pages of internal investigations [on me] out there."

Yes, this is the same man who found the Isotoner gloves and the tiny spots of blood in the dark, and entered O.J.'s property without a warrant. And 77 percent of white America still believes the Official Story.

2. The Rich and Famous Have Never Committed Capital Murder.

Don't get me wrong. The rich are the biggest murderers throughout history. But I'm not talking about killing in the abstract (like Kissinger being responsible for the deaths of countless Vietnamese and Cambodians, or the Ford Motor Company producing Pintos they knew might explode on impact); I mean actual, with-your-own-hands, thought-out-in-advance capital murder.

Can you think of a single rich, famous celebrity in the history of this country who has committed first-degree murder?

Go ahead, I'm waiting. And don't give me *relatives* of celebrities, like Marlon Brando's *son* (he killed his sister's boyfriend in a fight), Andy Williams's *wife* (Claudine Longet divorced Andy and then "accidentally" killed Olympic skier Spider Sabich), Lana Turner's *daughter* (Cheryl stabbed Lana's abusive boyfriend, Johnny Stompanato, when he was threatening her), Fatty Arbuckle (a victim of William Randolph Hearst's smear campaign, Fatty was found innocent), John du Pont (who was certainly rich but not a celebrity, and completely unknown outside the wrestling community when he killed Dave Schultz), or Sid Vicious (a doped-up

Brit who got a room in the Chelsea Hotel where he offed girlfriend Nancy and then killed himself).

I want you to name an actual American celebrity (not their relative) who is a multimillionaire and who, not in the "heat of the moment," but with cold-blooded planning, murdered another human being.

The truth is, *there isn't one.* Trust me, this is the safest group of people to be around. Put me on a subway car full of these fat cats any day! Force me to live in a tenement high-rise with the heads of Disney and Paramount and their top box office stars and I'll never lock my doors! You never have to be in fear of your life in their presence because *they* would never risk losing the lifestyle to which they've grown so accustomed.

Of course, the rich and famous do a lot of despicable things—cheat, lie, steal, do drugs, commit suicide, beat their wives, abandon their kids, take all the good parking spaces— but the one crime they *never* commit is premeditated murder.

Why? *Because they would have to get their hands dirty!*

If there is one thing I've learned in my brief Hollywood career, it's that these people *never* get their hands dirty. They do not do a damn thing for themselves. I mean *nothing.* They have so much money sitting around that they never have to lift a finger. Whether, as *The New Republic* points out, it's Pia Zadora having her assistant shave her armpits, or Liz Taylor boasting she has never set foot in a bank, or Henry Kissinger taking his dog for a walk and having his bodyguard walk behind him to scoop up the poop, or Bruce Willis requiring twenty-two personal assistants on the set of *Billy Bathgate,* these people never lift a finger to do anything. The list of "jobs" they hire others to do for them is amazing. You will never see a celebrity:

• **Pick up their dirty underwear.** A person in O.J.'s position has not done a load of laundry in years—if ever. He has never had to pick up his soiled Jockeys, strip his skanky bed, or wipe his snot off the wall.

- **Carry their own bags.** From the driver who picks him up at his house, to the "special services" personnel from the airlines who greet him at the curb, to the first-class flight attendants who lift his crap up into the overhead bin, O.J. has not had to carry anything but a nine-iron and a football in all his adult life.

- **Walk their dog.** In the building where I live in New York, each morning and evening a group of professional dog-walkers arrive to take the miniature poodles downstairs to deface our sidewalk. These dog-walkers earn a good living doing this.

- **De-grout their toenails.** I doubt O.J. has ever had some underpaid Mexican paint his toenails, and I'll bet he hasn't had to clean the gunk out from under any naillike surface on his body since moving to Brentwood.

- **Raise their kids.** Some celebrity couples have multiple nannies in the house who wake the kids in the morning, do their homework with them after school, and tuck them in at night. The parents will often call in their "good nights" on the phone in the child's room. Employees of the parents are sent to the private school to take notes and discuss their children's grades.

- **Do their shopping.** It was no accident that most of the presidential candidates this year didn't know how much a gallon of milk cost. These people haven't set foot inside a Safeway in decades. Remember George Bush at the check-out scanner? Just imagine these wealthy weenies trying to work an ATM machine!

- **Cook.** Why do that when you can get Kato to drive through McDonald's with you in your Rolls-Royce on the cook's day off?

- **Dial a phone number.** No matter which celebrities I have had meetings with in Hollywood, they will invariably yell out to an assistant, "Get so-and-so on the line for me!" I have never seen any of these people dial a telephone number on their own. If you want to see a blank stare, ask any of them to tell you their fax number.

- **Kill an ex-spouse.** If the rich actually get to the point where they feel compelled to eliminate the person they were once married to, they would *never, ever* do this job themselves—not when there are so many unemployed, desperate individuals around who are willing to off just about anyone for two hundred dollars. To do the job yourself would jeopardize your social position—and no matter how crazy you are, you're always sane enough to have this in the forefront of your mind. ("Rule Number One: I can do anything I want . . . except kill someone in cold blood with my own hands.")

The rich and famous are so removed from what the rest of us have to go through. Ask a celebrity to give his or her Zip Code. They can't. Ask them what the credit limit is on their MasterCard, and they'll say, "What's a MasterCard?" If they have any kind of credit card, it's the Platinum Card from American Express, which requires the holder to pay the entire amount charged at the end of every month. The rich have no need to carry a balance from month to month, paying only a bit at a time, like the rest of us schlumps.

If O.J. was involved with these murders (and I don't think he was), there is no way he committed them himself. Just as he paid a guy to wipe down his hot tub twice a week, he would have hired it done.

3. The Killer Was Smart, Not Stupid Like O.J.

Whoever committed this crime knew what they were doing. Next time you're in L.A., take a spin down Bundy on a Sunday evening in front of Nicole's condo. Man, this is one busy street! It's practically a major thoroughfare, connecting San Vicente and Wilshire. A car passes by her place about once every five seconds. People are out walking their dogs (Nicole lived in the downscale part of Brentwood, where residents walk their *own* dogs), and there is a lot of activity in the neighborhood around 10:00 P.M. The killer (or killers) pulled off a grisly double murder where one of the victims put up quite an intense struggle, and there was *not a single witness*. No murder weapon was ever recovered. No blood-soaked clothes (the slashing of Ron and Nicole spewed about two gallons of human blood out onto the killer and the crime scene) were ever found. This person (and his possible accomplice) knew exactly what he was doing.

Now take O.J. Simpson. The guy's day begins at 6:00 A.M. at the Riviera Country Club where he plays eighteen holes of golf. Later, after a few rounds of gin rummy in the clubhouse, he goes home, picks up his July issue of *Playboy,* and decides he has to talk to the centerfold, Traci Adell, whom he has never met. So he tracks her down in Maryland, where she's making a film, and they talk for forty-five minutes. ("He started talking about his ex-wives," she said later in an interview. "And he made a little joke about how I'm not his typical type. He said he'd dated blondes.") He stays on the phone with Traci for too long and, like a jerk, shows up late for his daughter's dance recital. He is videotaped afterward looking upbeat and happy, talking to Nicole and the kids. He later gets Kato to go to McDonald's with him. Now the guy is tanked up on a Big Mac and a large order of fries. He has to get ready and leave to go to the airport in less than an hour and a half.

So, if we are to believe the prosecution, he leaves himself only thirty minutes to drive over to Nicole's, commit the murders, and get back so he can shower, pack, and head off to LAX. To commit the murder, he doesn't take the weapon of choice among us nonprofessionals—the handgun (quick, easy, no bloodstains on your Ralph Lauren polo shirt). He takes a big knife!

Oh, and he forgets that he is black. Here we have a BLACK guy supposedly wandering around Brentwood on a busy street at night, wearing a black knit hat and black gloves, carrying a big knife. And, without anyone seeing him, he brutally and repeatedly stabs two strong, healthy young people only twenty-five feet from the street. He then gets rid of the knife and all the clothes, goes back home, showers, packs, and calmly gets into the limo for the ride to the airport, without a bruise on him.

I know O.J. is big and black, so that may be enough for some of you to believe the above is possible. God knows, we all shit a brick whenever we see a Big Black Guy walking toward us in the middle of the night!

But what if O.J. were white? Would you feel just the slightest bit different? If that incredible scenario had been told to you about, say, Frank Gifford or Marv Albert, would you be so quick to rush to judgment? Or if the victim had been O.J.'s first wife, a black woman, do you think this case would have received the same intense media attention and public outcry? Please, answer honestly.

4. I Always Lie to the Driver.

One of the perks that comes with working in Hollywood is The Car they send to pick you up. The first time this happened to me, after *Roger & Me* was released, I hopped into the *front* seat with the driver—which made him very nervous because the rules say you are to sit in the backseat while he drives you. When I got out, I went to pay him, and he laughed and said it was covered by the studio. If you are from the working class, you'll remember the embarrassment you experienced that first time you flew on a plane and, not knowing any better, got out your wallet to pay the stewardess for the meal.

These drivers, by and large, are a creepy bunch. I hate to say that because it's such a shitty job and I'm sure they're treated very poorly by the rich farts they drive around. But in the past year, on various trips to L.A., I have been subjected to a desperate Rupert Pupkin–type appeal by a driver to put him in my next film, an offer to join the Church of Scientology, two accidents, a driver who asked me to wait in the car while he went in to fence some "hot" jewelry, and a driver who chewed my ear off about having been arrested that morning for child abuse and how he was going to "hunt down that cunt of an ex-wife and teach her a thing or two." When he didn't return to pick me up, I was stranded alone, two hours from the city. I called the car service to tell them he had probably abandoned me so he could go back to beat up his ex-wife whom he called a "cunt."

"Well, sir," replied his boss, "she is." I told this moron that as long as women were treated in this manner, the world would not be safe for them. I then asked the studio the next day never to use this service again, and they agreed, costing the limo company, I hope, thousands of dollars of business.

Which brings me to Alan Park, O.J.'s driver on the night of the murders. The prosecution hailed him as their star witness. He testified that he just kept ringing the bell and there was no answer. There was no light on in the bedroom. Then he saw a black man going in the front door. (Marcia Clark says Park saw a man walk across the lawn, but Park never testified to this.) He said that he buzzed O.J. again, and O.J. told him over the intercom that he had overslept (O.J. denies this), and that he had just taken a shower.

Either way, "I was in the shower" is just one of those lies you tell the drivers who want you to come out and get in their car as soon as they get there. These drivers always show up a half hour early and bug the hell out of you because as soon as they can get rid of you they can make more money by squeezing in another pickup. My policy is never to answer their call until I'm ready to leave. And when I come down I always make up some weird excuse.

("Sorry, but I had Fidel Castro on the phone, and you know, you can never get him to shut up.") God help me if any of these drivers ever believe me or are called to testify against me. ("Yes, your honor, he was on the phone with Castro for hours and when he entered the limo he seemed fidgety and not entirely lucid.")

It turns out that, from where Park was sitting, he could not see the bedroom window because it was in the back of the house. Yes, that was O.J. walking in the front door—so what? Of course O.J. lied to him. That's what you're supposed to do with the driver.

5. Why the Cops Planted the Evidence.

In spite of the above-listed crimes committed by the LAPD, I do not believe the reason they planted the glove, socks, and blood was because they are evil. I honestly trust that they believed in their heart of hearts that O.J. committed these murders. But by 5:00 A.M., six hours after the murders, having combed the area for the weapon and waking neighborhood residents out of bed to try to find a witness, they knew that they were without a case. They also knew that O.J., in the past, had beaten Nicole, so it was more than likely he was the prime suspect. But, they probably surmised, this guy was rich and famous and would definitely beat the rap, so they knew they had to strengthen their hand against a judicial system they perceived as unfair.

So a glove mysteriously turns up at the murder site *and* on the side of O.J.'s house. Though blood-soaked, it picks up no dirt or leaves from the ground. Apparently, O.J. was sneaking around the back of his house and the glove—a rather tight-fitting glove, as we saw at the trial—just fell off his hand and dried itself on the way to the ground so that no dirt would stick to it.

Then O.J. apparently went into his house, which is filled with white carpet. To avoid getting bloodstains on this carpet (none were discovered), he either put on a jet pack and flew upstairs to his bedroom, or had some Totes handy near the front door, which he slipped on and then got rid of later. Once in the bedroom, he found a way to dispose of all of his clothes except his socks and, like most guys, left them right out in the open for someone to pick up—like the L.A. police.

None of O.J.'s blood was found on Nicole's gate the night of the murder, but somehow I guess O.J. was able to sneak out of the L.A. County Jail and go back there and bleed all over the gate, because two weeks later, on July 3, a spot of O.J.'s blood suddenly appeared on that gate and was photographed by the police. I have heard of this happening to statues of the Blessed Virgin in various churches throughout the world, but I had never considered the spiritual powers of O.J.

I'm sure that Detective VanAtter meant to walk two doors down the hall to turn O.J.'s blood over to the lab after it was drawn from The Juice, but he got distracted, dropped the blood sample in his pocket, and headed out twenty miles to the crime scene. An honest mistake, just like when 1.5 cc of that blood came up missing. Probably the humidity in VanAtter's pocket—a place I'd never want to see the inside of—caused the stuff to evaporate.

There is a logical explanation for everything—just as there had to be when the L.A. cops planted evidence in these cases:

• Sylvester Scott was arrested in March 1987 after Los Angeles sheriff's deputies left a plastic bag filled with cocaine inside his car during a search. Scott testified at the L.A. Sheriff's Department corruption trials of the early 1990s.

Former sheriff Robert Sobel also testified that on four or five occasions, deputies stole cocaine that had been stored as evidence and replaced it with a substance resembling cocaine, then planted the cocaine in the homes or cars of individuals they wanted to arrest.

Thirty members of the L.A. Sheriff's Department have been federally prosecuted for planting evidence, writing false police reports, and using excessive force against suspects.

• In the case of Clarence Chance, police coerced witnesses into manufacturing evidence against him. As a result, he was convicted of and wrongly served more than seventeen years in jail for a murder he did not commit.

This little trick of planting the goods is not unique to L.A.:

• The Mollen Commission, which spent twenty-two months investigating police corruption in New York City, concluded in a 1994 report that falsification of evidence and perjury were probably the most common types of police corruption facing the city's criminal justice system.

• In 1995, more than fifteen New York City police officers in Harlem's 30th Precinct were indicted for or pleaded guilty to falsifying evidence or lying about how or where they found evidence. Subsequently, about 125 defendants were cleared of wrongdoing. Among themselves, officers nicknamed this widespread practice "testilying."

• New York State troopers were recently convicted of participating in an evidence-tampering scheme that involved planting fingerprints at crime scenes to falsely implicate suspects.

• In 1995, in Philadelphia, six police officers pleaded guilty to corruption charges, including planting false evidence and lying under oath. This has resulted in overturning more than **sixty** criminal cases, including that of a fifty-four-year-old grandmother imprisoned for three years after police officers planted narcotics in her row house.

6. That White Ford Bronco.

Ninety million people are tuned in to watch the performance of a white Ford Bronco during a police chase—and the thing can't go over forty miles per hour?! Pity the poor executives at Ford, back in Detroit, watching this abomination on national TV and screaming at the tube, "*Step on it, Juice!*"

I wonder how many people know about the prosecution's internal memo—not released until after the jury's verdict—that confirmed that they knew O.J. and Al Cowlings had gone to Nicole's grave on that Bronco ride (the police traced O.J.'s cellular phone and learned that he was at the cemetery).

And why was it we didn't find out until after the trial, from the same prosecutor's memo, that Al Cowlings actually pulled the Bronco over on the freeway when the first police cars arrived behind him? When Cowlings got out and saw that the police were drawing their guns, he dove back into the Bronco and took off. Why was this information withheld?

And what about the passport, the money, the gun, and the disguise? A lot of people I know, including myself, always carry their passports in their briefcases or purses—hey, you never know! The rich always carry a *huge* wad of money on them, and half of this country (myself not included) is packing heat. And the disguise? Hey, I never said O.J. wasn't weird. Maybe it was just tossed in the back of the Bronco from his last date with a *Playboy* centerfold.

7. If You Had Killed Someone and the Jury Miraculously Let You Off, Would You Be Calling In to Every Talk Show and Acting Like a Jerk?

Hell, no, I'd be out of Dodge like a lightning bolt, counting my blessings. You would never hear a peep from me again. But if I were truly innocent, and the majority of the country still didn't believe me after a jury of my peers said that I was, I might be acting a little crazy, too. If you've seen O.J.'s video or his appearance on Black Entertainment Television, you'd have to pause and wonder if just maybe he didn't commit these crimes. If you have an open mind, his evidence and explanation are quite convincing.

8. Look at Who's Whining About Playing the "Race Card"!

So Johnnie Cochran played the "race card." From what deck was this card dealt? From the one we white people stacked! We knew exactly what Cochran was doing because we've been dealing that card on Black America their entire lives. The deck is, and always has been, stacked against O.J. and every other person whose skin color isn't white. I couldn't have been happier to see Johnnie Cochran talk directly to the black jurors and remind them that the oppressive system that assaults them every day is the same system that constantly plants evidence, lies, and frames black citizens to the point where nearly half a million of them are behind bars in this country.

The only reason O.J. isn't one of them is that he had the money to fight it. People complain that O.J. got off because he was rich. In fact, his wealth was only an equalizer that somewhat leveled the playing field in the courtroom. The prosecution *always* has more money and resources than the defense; even in this case, the DA spent more than the defense. O.J. Simpson's wealth was his only hope to make up for the fact that he was black.

People went crazy when Johnnie Cochran compared the Idaho-bound Mark Fuhrman's attitude to that which brought about the Holocaust. Well, why the hell not? I believe it is our responsibility to shout down bigotry and racism wherever it exists, especially when it involves those who propose a "final solution." (Remember witness Kathleen Bell? She said Fuhrman told her about wanting to round up all blacks and set fire to them.) We dishonor the memory of the Holocaust and its victims whenever we stand silent and allow this type of hatred to go unchecked.

It is more than ironic that O.J. spent most of his life sucking up to the white establishment, playing golf with them, making sure most of his friends were white, living with them in Brentwood, marrying one of them, and exclusively dating them after his divorce.

O.J., if you are reading this, I have to say you tried harder than any black man I know to be one of us—AND A LOT OF FUCKING GOOD THAT DID YOU! Within hours of the first TV report on the murders, you, The Most Loved Black Man in White America, were suddenly booted back to the ghetto faster than you can say H. Rap Brown. God, it must have been awful, all those years of smiling at the country club while listening to really stupid, racist white people. All those years of trying to make sure that those white people you were around felt relaxed enough in your presence. They let you sit on their corporate boards, they let you into the best restaurants in town—and in an instant, they took it all away from you.

And now, even after all this, you're still trying to please them. Look at you, promising now to go out and find the real killer. Hey, that's *their* job. What you *should* be doing is getting some help, 'cause you've got a real problem with women. I hear there are a lot of good shrinks in L.A.—or maybe you shouldn't wait. Just pick up the phone and call me (you can get my number from your former agent who is also my former agent). Or try the Alternatives to Violence Program at (310) 493-1161. They are especially equipped to help men like you who mistake women for a doormat.

As for the rest of us, O.J., I guess we share the collective guilt of not punishing you for beating Nicole. Each time she called 911, our representatives (the police) would show up at your door, say, "Hey, Juice," give you a pat on the back, get your autograph, and leave. The one time you actually got dragged into court, you got a $700 fine and "community service." You call that "paying your dues"? Really? How 'bout if I came over tonight and beat the crap out of your daughter until she's so black and blue she can't shut her right eye? Would seven hundred bucks and a little community service sit okay with you? Think about how that would feel next time you open your mouth about "all this nonsense" regarding battered women.

Did you commit those murders? I don't think so. But you have helped the nation confront a number of ugly truths about itself and reminded us, once again, that we still live in two separate Americas—one white, the other black. For that, I, and even those who are sure of your guilt, are grateful.

The "Liddy Problem"

MEMO TO: Republican National Committee
FROM: Haley Barbour, Chairman, Republican Party
RE: THE "LIDDY PROBLEM"

As you all know, one of our most successful disinformation campaigns of the past four years has been convincing the majority of Americans that Hillary Clinton is the Number One Dyke-on-Wheels/Bitch from Hell. How we pulled this off without the help of the dearly deceased Lee Atwater (he gave us Willie Horton, then turned traitor on us before his last gasp), I'll never understand.

I mean, here you have Mrs. Rodham-Clinton, who in real life is active in the Methodist Church, quits her job to raise her daughter, and stays at home to help her husband like any good Republican woman would do—and we got the American public believing she's running the country from Communist Party headquarters!

CHAPTER 26

(Did you know that she even had a *kitchen* put into the living quarters in the upstairs of the White House so the three of them could sit around the table, cook, and talk—just like a *family*? How did we ever prevent that wholesome story from getting out? Sometimes you just gotta believe God *is* on our side!)

Well, now, I don't want to sound any alarms, but I think it's best that we prepare ourselves for that dreaded day when the media catch on to Liddy Dole. So far, she's been able to pull off looking like the anti-Hillary with that Southern charm thing she does.

But all it's gonna take is just one femi-nazi journalist to get the ball rolling—and then we're going to have some explaining to do.

These are where I see the main problem areas:

1. Senator Dole is a divorced man. He dumped his first wife, who had stood by him all the way through his career. Before you could say "Bring me a younger babe!" he clicked his heels together three times and it was back to Kansas for ol' Phyllis Dole.

So, in 1975, the year before he runs as vice president with Ford, he marries Elizabeth "Liddy" Hanford—and she's twelve years younger than him. Man, she sure was a looker! I can see why the geezer went after her. But none of this will play well with our "family values" theme, so see if you can come up with a better explanation than Gingrich did when he brought his sick wife the divorce papers and dumped them on her hospital bed.

2. The Doles have no children. It's probably too late to get them started, so the least said about this, the better. Should anyone raise the obvious question, "How does Dole know what the average family is going through when he doesn't have one?"—send their name to our head of security and we will do a background check.

Also, I understand Dole has a daughter from his first marriage—but we never see her. Is there any way to make her more visible (say, bookings on "Jenny Jones" or "Politically Incorrect") *without* drawing attention to the fact that she is the spawn of the first wife?

3. The Doles don't live in a house—they live in the Watergate! Multiple problems here. What the hell is he doing inside the place that brought our party to near ruin? It's bad enough he sorta looks like Nixon. And, once again, the Doles *don't live like most Americans.* They live in some kind of condo/hotel suite, for chrissakes! While most Americans are switching to Hamburger Helper to make ends meet, these two are dialing up room service from Howard Hunt!

Get the two of them out of there immediately. Take some "soft money" from our Miscellaneous Fund and buy them a three-bedroom wood frame house in suburban Maryland and another one just like it in Russell, Kansas, where he's supposed to be from. (Note to those handling this: Make sure there's one of those big American flags you see outside of car dealerships flying in front of both homes.)

4. Hillary went to an Ivy League school; Liddy went to an Ivy League school. Hillary is a lawyer; Liddy is a lawyer. Hillary has worked all her adult life; Liddy has worked all her adult life, *and* she has held top positions in presidential cabinets, corporate boards, and national organizations. How can we go on attacking Hillary, when Liddy is more "Hillary" than Hillary?

• • •

I am alerting you to these problems only as a means to prepare ourselves for any potential catastrophe. The media may be a lazy, compliant bunch, and the American public may be as stupid as junkyard dogs—but they ain't this stupid. I fear we may have our nuts in the wringer if we don't head the enemy off at the pass.

Keep the focus on Hillary as much as possible. Make sure Liddy appears at *all* natural disasters with her Red Cross helmet on.

With God on our side, we will weather the storm.

EYES ONLY.

I Try to Commit
Bob Dornan

THERE ARE A LOT of nutty characters who hold seats in our Congress. There's a group of five or six of them who refuse to get a place in D.C. and sleep each night on cots in their Capitol Hill offices just to prove they'll never "go Washington."

Then there's Representative Gerald Solomon. He started screaming from the floor of the House one day about the need to repeal the ban on assault weapons because his wife was living all alone in the woods in upstate New York and she had the right to have an Uzi under her pillow.

CHAPTER 27

And who can forget Representative Enid Waldholtz from Utah? She had no idea who her husband really was and what he did with her money. Or how about Congresswoman Helen Chenowith from Idaho? She believes that the UN is flying "black helicopters" over militia compounds in the Northwest, preparing for a UN invasion.

A lot of wackiness, to be sure, but nothing that any of them says or does comes close to the actions of one Representative Robert K. Dornan of Orange County, California. Nicknamed "B-1 Bob" for both his support of the bomber built in his district and his onetime acting stint on TV's "Twelve O'Clock High" series, Dornan has physically assaulted a member of Congress and has threatened the President. He rants like a mad dog on the floor of the House about "homos" and a "disloyal, betraying little Jew."

He seems to be convinced that the communist conspiracy is alive and well—in the Democratic Party! He once personally investigated Ted Kennedy's accident at Chappaquiddick by swimming the channel to prove that Kennedy was lying about what happened that night his car rolled off the bridge and Mary Jo Kopechne died.

All of this nuttiness culminated in 1996 when Bob Dornan entered the Republican presidential race. At his announcement, he warned about what he saw as his fate on the campaign trail:

"I'll probably die with my boots on . . . [but] I want to go down swinging," Dornan told the media.

What made Bob Dornan think he was qualified to be President of the United States? *Los Angeles Times* columnist Dana Parsons put together a list of things that Dornan has personally informed him that he has accomplished:

- He set a transcontinental speed record from the Caribbean to California in 1957 in an F-100D Super Sabre.

- He flew more than three times the speed of sound in an SR-71 Blackbird spy reconnaissance aircraft.

- He was clocked at 135.7 mph in a competition speed-boat.

- He argued with the head of the KGB in Moscow.

- He escaped, by *one day*, an assassination attempt in Burma.

- He was trapped in rioting in Warsaw in 1988.

- He is an accomplished impersonator and at one time had a polished stand-up act.

- He was one of the first people on the scene of Howard Hughes's plane crash in Beverly Hills in 1946.

- He was one of the first people on the scene of the assassination of gangster Bugsy Siegel.

Bob Dornan is also the nephew of Jack Haley, who played the Tin Man in *The Wizard of Oz*.

During his first term in Congress, Dornan warned his colleagues that Soviet KGB agents were probably watching the proceedings from the visitors' galleries. He once stormed into a Catholic church rectory in Orange County and denounced the bishops as Communists. He has stomped on a North Vietnamese flag during a debate with Vietnam veteran and antiwar activist Ron Kovic, and once burned Jane Fonda in effigy on the USC campus.

Dornan also has a history of alleged spousal abuse. Between 1960 and 1976, his wife, Sallie, filed for divorce *four times*. Her lawsuits contained graphic descriptions of physical abuse. In the first case, in 1961, Sallie claimed Bob "dragged her about the home . . . by her hair . . . and exhibited a revolver." She also claimed Dornan poured a quart of milk over her head. She has since recanted these claims, saying she was on prescription drugs when she made them.

In 1966, Dornan was held in violation of a restraining order based on his "violent attack on his wife." Dornan was sentenced to jail, but never served time.

In 1985, Dornan called fellow congressman Tom Downey a "draft-dodging wimp" and a "liar." When Downey approached Dornan in the House chamber and asked Dornan if he had said those things, Dornan wheeled around and snarled, "Yeah, so what?" Then he started to lose control. Eyes bulging, he grabbed Downey by his necktie and jerked him around, yelling at him, "Don't let me catch you off the Floor, where you're protected by a sergeant at arms." He yanked Downey closer to his face and screamed, "Stay out of my face, now and forever!"

Is Bob Dornan mental? Is he a ticking time bomb waiting to explode? Consider these statements he's made, and ask yourself if this man isn't crying out for help:

> "Defining patriotism to you [President Clinton] is like explaining Judaism to Hitler. From the abortion of young children to euthanasia of the elderly to your health care plan, life is secondary to your thirst for power."

• • •

> "I used to pine away that my birthday wasn't April 13. That was Thomas Jefferson's birthday. . . . Until I discovered that [my birthday] of April 3 was the day that Christ was crucified."

• • •

> ". . . Roosevelt's birthday is January 30. Hitler was sworn in on Roosevelt's birthday. . . . And then Roosevelt was sworn in on March 4. Well, my mother was eight months pregnant [with me]. . . . Now, I'm not being

spooky about it, I'm just saying within a month of Roosevelt ['s inauguration]—I'm born! ... The world really took off while I'm in my mother's womb."

• • •

"If you look at the predicates to last year, it was Woody Allen's woody, it was Pee-Wee's wee pee-pee. When did Prince Charlie want to turn his scepter into a tampon? Was that last year—the year of *Free Willy?* ... If you think about this, as not 'The Year of the Dog,' but as 'The Year of the Penis'; the Bobbitts; the Ventura police photographing King Michael's white willy—assuming he's bleached himself everywhere. And ending up with four state troopers talking about Slick Willy's willy. . . . The whole year has been about nothing but private parts."

• • •

Regarding men in the pro-choice movement: "They are either women trapped in men's bodies like Alan Alda or Phil Donahue, or younger guys who are like camp followers looking for easy sex."

• • •

". . . 'homosexual.' To shorten it to 'homo' may have a cruel ring, like shortening 'Japanese' to 'Jap.' It worked during the Second World War, it's not considered polite . . . but use the word."

• • •

"Every lesbian spearchucker in this country is hoping I get defeated."

• • •

"We have a rep on our side who is a homo who goes in and out of the closet."

• • •

On gays' attraction to thighs: "Oh, I've been hit on. And always the same ridiculous line: 'Boy, you have nice thighs.'" Also: "[Clinton] is jogging in San Francisco in his slit-up-the-sides silk girlie-girlie jogging pants, showing us those beautiful white doughboy thighs of his."

• • •

Concerned about Dornan's mental state, I decided to consult a psychiatrist to see if a professional concurred with my opinion. Although the first two shrinks I called said that he showed signs of "impulse control disorder," "intermittent explosive disorder," and "paranoid personality," they did not want to go on the record for fear that someone in Dornan's position (or mental state) would come after them.

I then placed an anonymous call to a couple of psychiatric clinics in suburban Virginia, where Dornan resides. Without mentioning the name of the individual I was describing, I shared the above information with them. They were both quite concerned.

"It sounds like he's having some type of psychotic break," a psychiatric nurse at the Charter Behavioral Health System at Springwood told me. "It sounds like he needs to get in for some type of evaluation."

I asked her to describe for me exactly what the term "psychotic" meant.

"A psychotic," she explained, "is a person that's having some type of mental situation where they're out of touch with reality. . . . It could be a chemical imbalance in his brain and then he would have to be put on some medication to counteract that. . . . It certainly isn't going to go away by itself."

She said that if I "feel in danger, [you need] to call the police and get them involved. If he were to become out of control . . . in a public place, you need to inform his friends that they need to call the police . . . if the police get involved, then he'll be forced to [come in for treatment]."

She asked me if he was hearing voices in his head. I told her that he thinks rock-and-roll albums contain hidden Satanic messages, audible only when played backwards.

"Well, there is rock and roll that has Satanic messages that you can hear when you play it backwards," the nurse said matter-of-factly. "That is true."

Feeling that I may have called the wrong treatment center, I tried the psychiatric wing at Dominion Hospital in Falls Church. The nurse on duty, after hearing the circumstances of the "anonymous" individual, stated, "This man certainly sounds like he is mentally ill." She explained the process I would have to go through to get Dornan committed.

First, the police would bring him to the hospital, and they would get a temporary detaining order. Then there would be a hearing at the hospital with a special justice from the district court. Dornan would be provided with a court-appointed attorney and a court psychologist. The court would then decide if he was to be released or placed in treatment, depending on what type of insurance he had.

I checked with an attorney in Virginia who read for me the relevant state code defining *mentally ill:*

Section 37.1-1: "Any person afflicted with mental disease to such extent that for his own welfare or for the welfare of others, he requires care and treatment."

There was no doubt this definition applied to Robert Dornan. For his own welfare, and the welfare of others, he must be put away. So I had my assistant call the Mobile Crisis Unit hot line at the Woodburne Community Health Center in Fairfax, Virginia.

I'd like to request a pickup of a disturbed citizen.
What's the client's name?

The client's name is Robert Dornan.
Is he a Woodburne Center client? I recognize that name.

I don't know that he is. He actually may be.
How old is he?

In his fifties. I don't know exactly . . . He rants and raves quite a bit in public. He talks a lot about enemies, perceived enemies. He has made threats. He's actually physically attacked people in a public place. He has made violent outbursts. He has said very nasty, threatening things about gay people, about Jews. He has this thing about numerology. He wishes his birthday was on Thomas Jefferson's birthday. . . . He thinks there is something significant about the fact that Hitler was sworn in on Roosevelt's birthday. . . . He has gone into Catholic rectories and denounced the bishops as communists . . . wife abuse . . . He needs to be evaluated, and I don't think he'll ever do it on his own.
Will she [his wife] call and make the report?

No, I don't think so.
What is your relationship to him?

I'm just a person who has witnessed his behavior—not close up, but from afar.
Well, one of the things that I should tell you about is that if Mobile Crisis comes out and he needs to be detained, there needs to be someone there who has witnessed the behavior.

I've witnessed the behavior. Not in person, but on videotape.
On videotape. How do you see it on videotape?

He's actually a public figure.
[Long pause.]
Well, I guess what I recommend is that you call Mobile Crisis after tomorrow, see if they would be willing to take the case.

If you actually took the van out to his house, what would you do?
We always have the option of involving the police. If we think there is a danger issue, that's likely. And I suspect if it's the same Robert Dornan that I think you are speaking of, that they are going to want to take the police because he is a public figure. I sure would, if I were going.

Do you think since he is a public figure that they might be reluctant to pursue this?
Not if there are grounds to do it. They are probably going to approach it carefully.

Do you agree that Bob Dornan needs some help?
I know of Representative Dornan and I know a bit about his public behavior, but I wouldn't conclude from that he needs a mental health assessment.

• • •

Where does that leave us with B-1 Bob? Unprotected! The authorities refuse to see what is so clear to me. I can only offer my sincerest warning to the members of the House who must work with him daily, to his family and friends, and to the innocent children who live on his block in Fairfax, Virginia—BEWARE OF BOB!! Watch your back. And, for God's sake, try to persuade him to seek help immediately!

• • •

The following letter was sent by Representative Bob Dornan to Michael Farber, the Democratic opponent he defeated in his 1994 congressional race, and Farber's wife:

Congress of the United States
House of Representatives
Washington, DC 20515–2201

Dear Michael and Gail,

. . . I think the only thing you are devoted to, Mike, is yourself. Doesn't bode well for your marriage. Remember what I told you about the Pharaoh's curse: <u>Five out of five</u> of my married opponents <u>divorced, all within months</u> after I defeated them. . . .

In closing, Mike and Gail, I have always found it interesting that all of my political opponents who have run smear campaigns against me have this peculiar propensity for disappearing off the political <u>and public life</u> radar screen . . . FOREVER. Which doesn't say much for your future prospects, I'm afraid. But then it will give you ample time for reflextion and soul-saving—starting with your own.

<u>Devoutly</u> yours,
ROBERT K. DORNAN

Skip the Candidates—
Vote for the Lobbyists!

POLITICIANS. WE LOVE to hate them. And they make it so easy for us. But should they be the true objects of our scorn? I mean, how much power do they *really* have?

As most of us know, very little. Maybe that's another reason why a lot of people don't vote: the real power, the men and women who actually call the shots, are nowhere to be found on the ballot.

CHAPTER 28

If Toto could pull back the curtain of Congress for us, what we would see is a bunch of powerful men who are pulling the levers. These Wizards of Oz in Washington are called lobbyists. Although we can't see them, they are there every day, making sure that Congress does exactly what Corporate America wants it to. To cement this relationship, the lobbyists provide a lot of cash to these politicians, guaranteeing that they will do their bidding.

After the Republicans took over in the 1994 elections, they told the lobbyists that they could come out from hiding and help them undo decades of social programs, environmental regulations, and other federal activities that have hampered Big Business. They asked lobbyists representing 350 various corporate interests actually to write key provisions of the Contract With America, to sit in on congressional meetings, and even to move right into *our* Congress. An executive from Dow Chemical took a leave of absence from his job at Dow and went to work for free on the House Commerce Committee!

If the lobbyists are just going to set up shop right on the floor of the House and Senate and direct the legislation that is to be passed, isn't it just a waste of time for us to go to the polls and elect the middleman politicians—especially when we could be voting for the *real deal* in the first place? If the lobbyists are calling the shots, why not just elect *them*? It's more honest that way. We'll know exactly what we're getting. And it's more *democratic*, don't you think, since the lobbyists are the people really running the show?

To that end, I am calling for all of us on election day to write in the names of the real representatives in Congress. If you don't already know who the lobbyist is that owns your congressman or senator, let me provide you with a few examples of some of the districts I've been following.

MIKE'S CANDIDATES
FOR A MORE REALISTIC CONGRESS

VERN CLARK

Our candidate for Pennsylvania's Ninth Congressional District, currently occupied by Republican Congressman Bud Shuster, Chairman of the House Transportation and Infrastructure Committee.

Vern Clark, a legendary lobbyist in Washington, represents the billboard industry, one of the smallest yet most influential industries lobbying Congress today. Vern is famous for his dispensation of political contributions, honoraria, and junkets. Back in 1987, Washington's *Regardies* magazine called him one of the most powerful unelected men on Capitol Hill. And he still is—powerful *and* unelected!

The billboard lobby is an interest group that has *lots* of money. That's why Vern's been so effective. He's been able to steer the gradual dismantling of the 1965 Highway Beautification Act (Lady Bird Johnson's pet project). This act was supposed to end the clutter of billboards along our federal highways.

In 1991, when the Senate passed an amendment deleting antibillboard provisions from the highway bill, opponent Senator John Chafee (R-R.I.) said, "Vern Clark earned his pay today." A Senate aide told the *National Journal*, "Of all the things I've ever worked on, this is the most backroom, old-style type of lobbying. It's all hundred-dollar bills in blank envelopes."

No congressman has been a bigger ally of Vern's than Congressman Bud Shuster (R-Pa.). Just recently, Shuster fought hard for a provision in the 1995 highway bill, signed by President Clinton, that would allow more billboards on scenic byways. During 1994, Bud received $57,415 from the billboard industry. Asked by *U.S. News & World Report* about the $77,850 in billboard industry campaign contributions he has received since January 1991, Shuster said, "I am the darling of the billboard industry."

But why bother with the darling Bud Shuster when you can just get the real thing in Vern? Let's give Bud a rest. He's run unopposed for office since 1984, when he defeated "Beverly Hillbillies" actress Nancy Kulp.

So, if you live in the greater Altoona, Pennsylvania, area, please vote for Vern Clark for Congress.

WAYNE R. LAPIERRE JR.

Our candidate for the U.S. Senate, state of Texas, a seat currently occupied by Republican Senator Phil Gramm.

Wayne LaPierre is the executive vice president of the National Rifle Association (NRA), one of the most powerful lobbying organizations in history, according to the Center for Public Integrity in Washington. As Senator Gramm's largest single career sponsor, the NRA has already funneled $440,200 to him since 1979, more money than to any other politician in the United States during this period. Wayne himself recently attended a thousand-dollar-a-plate dinner for Phil Gramm in Dallas, which raised $4.1 million for his now defunct presidential campaign.

In return, Gramm has introduced, sponsored, or voted on eighteen key NRA-supported bills. In 1987 and 1989, he co-chaired the Annual Charlton Heston International Celebrity Shoot, attracting such celebrities as O. J. Simpson and Arnold Schwarzenegger. The money, according to the Center for Public Integrity, went to the NRA's Institute for Legislative Action (i.e., NRA lobbying). And he's solicited money for the NRA on the NRA's own stationery.

But what's the point of all this? Why should the NRA waste their money on a middleman like Gramm? What does Phil Gramm do that Wayne LaPierre couldn't do more directly, and more efficiently?

Wayne LaPierre, forty-six years old, became one of the NRA's best-known figures after the Oklahoma City bombing, when he wrote a fund-raising letter characterizing the Bureau of Alcohol, Tobacco and Firearms agents as "jack-booted government thugs." This led NRA lifetime member George Bush to resign in disgust. Wayne is also a speed reader and an author. His book, *Guns, Crime, and Freedom*, has sold more than 275,000 copies in hardcover, and is now in paperback.

He seems to have the right experience and temperament for Washington. Josh Sugarman, head of the antigun Violence Policy Center, says, "I call [Wayne] the Ringo Starr of the NRA; he was at the right place at the right time for that job."

According to the Gannett News Service, Wayne spends one-third of the year on the road, averaging 100 speeches. Let's keep him off the highway and in Washington where he belongs. Vote Wayne in '96!

ROBERT G. LIBERATORE

Our candidate for the Sixteenth District of Michigan, currently held by Congressman John Dingell, ranking Democrat, House Committee on Commerce.

Robert Liberatore is Chrysler's chief lobbyist in Washington. Like the rest of the auto industry, Chrysler has its best congressional friend in John Dingell. Ralph Nader once called Dingell "a national menace," the "disgrace from Dearborn," and "the number one enemy to consumers on Capitol Hill" (and that was Ralph on a happy day). Dingell was a vehement opponent of air bags, a position shared by Chrysler and the rest of the auto industry for years.

Since his election in 1955, Representative Dingell has been the auto industry's literal voice in Congress. Whether it's his opposition to air pollution controls, safety regulations, or better gas mileage, Dingell has always been there for the auto lobbyists. And they've been there for him, too. In fact, he married one of them. Debbie Dingell, or "my little wife Debbie," as he calls her, was a lobbyist for GM when they met. Debbie is a Fisher Body heiress and still works for the company. In 1991, Congressman Dingell led forty members of Congress to Detroit to hear the Big Three auto chiefs complain about economic problems and the cost of government regulations. Debbie arranged the trip's schedule.

Dingell says, "I think the credibility of the automobile industry is splendid. The problem is, nobody else does." His latest favor for Chrysler came in the form of a letter to the National Highway Transportation and Safety Administration (NHTSA), in the middle of a controversial fight over what should be done about 3.9 million 1984–94 defective Chrysler minivans. The door latches in these vans would fail during crashes, allowing passengers to be ejected out the rear hatch. Auto safety advocates had demanded a recall.

On January 17, 1995, in the midst of this debate, Dingell and Representative Michael Oxley (R-Ohio) wrote a letter to NHTSA expressing concern about its policies and procedures for determining defects and recalls, expressing heavy congressional "interest" in this, as NHTSA was up for reauthorization. Shortly after the letter was sent, NHTSA decided not to order a Chrysler minivan recall.

Dingell says, "Protecting the automobile industry has always been a very difficult and very necessary task that I have had to undertake." Why burden him with this job any longer? Wouldn't it be easier with a representative from Chrysler right there in office?

Robert Liberatore is the perfect candidate, credited for giving Chrysler its "very active Washington presence." He's got the revolving-door experience. Before coming to Chrysler in 1985, he worked on Capitol Hill for ten years, including a position as staff director for Senate leader Robert C. Byrd. We've had John Dingell for forty-two years. Why put up with this surrogate one more year?

Fellow Michiganders, elect Robert Liberatore for Congress!

RICHARD E. WILEY

Our candidate for the U.S. Senate, state of South Dakota, currently occupied by Republican Senator Larry Pressler, chairman of the Senate Commerce Committee.

South Dakota Republican Senator Larry Pressler says he may well be the most lobbied senator in American history. Why? Because as chairman of the Senate Commerce Committee, Pressler was architect of the Telecommunications Act of 1995, considered the most lobbied bill ever. This new law reinvented communications in this country. It was "manna from heaven" for D.C. lobbyists, according to one congressman.

But it was also manna from heaven for Senator Larry Pressler. As soon as he became chairman of the Commerce Committee in 1994, Pressler started raking in major bucks from the telecommunications industry. Since then, according to *The Nation,* he's gotten over $163,000 in contributions from PACs associated with this industry and $163,887 from individuals working for connected firms.

In fact, he's the Senate's leading collector of 1995 PAC dollars. His Federal Election Commission (FEC) report shows that he raised a total of $962,468 as of August 1995, "nearly double the total amount he received over the last four years and almost thirty times the amount he received in 1979, his first year in Congress," according to the *Aberdeen American News.*

Consumer groups strongly opposed the communications bill because cable companies will soon be able to bill consumers whatever they want. As a result, cable rates will rise. In addition to allowing more and more of our media to be bought up by huge conglomerates, the bill also regulates "porn" on the Internet and requires the V-chip in new TV sets.

Some of the credit for its passage must go to one of the bill's principal lobbyists, former FCC chairman Richard Wiley. Wiley successfully represented both broadcasters and the newspaper industry, winning concessions from the powerful "Baby Bells." For example, the bill prevents the Baby Bells from having a competitive advantage over newspapers in electronic publishing.

Wiley is the quintessential "insider" lobbyist on telecommunications matters, given his prominent history with the FCC. Even before he was FCC chairman from 1974 to 1977, he was an FCC commissioner from 1972 to 1974 and FCC general counsel between 1970 and 1972. And he's the chairman of the FCC's Advisory Committee on Advanced TV Service.

Richard Wiley is clearly more appropriate for the Senate post than Pressler, about whom his South Dakota colleague Senator Tom Daschle once said, "A Senate seat is a terrible thing to waste."

Let's not waste it anymore. Let's elect Richard Wiley to the Senate!

● ● ●

These are just a few examples of who should really be running for office. Find out who owns your member of Congress and write his name in on the ballot. It's the only democratic thing to do.

Harassing Gays
for Extra Credit

THIS IS A STORY about a school in Topeka, Kansas, and how hard the students there work to get good grades.

Sam Phelps is one of those students. He's a good kid, comes from a good family. His grandfather is a preacher.

Topeka West High School encourages its students to go beyond just the "book learnin'" and explore activities in the community that could give them

CHAPTER 29

an enriching learning experience. The school recognizes the importance of what can be learned outside the school walls, and seeks to reward those students who enhance their knowledge.

So the kids leave school at 2:55 every afternoon and, instead of going home to watch Ricki Lake, they go to the senior citizens' center to help the old folks. Or to the hospital to help the disabled.

Or to carry a picket sign that reads DEATH TO FAGS at the funeral of someone who has just died of AIDS.

That's what Sam Phelps does for his Topeka West High community service. And his family joins him in his picketing. When they're not attending the funerals of AIDS victims, they harass gays at Barry Manilow concerts and publicly "out" local judges and officials who they believe are gay. "God hates fags," says Sam. "That is why God destroyed Sodom and Gomorrah—'cause they were anal copulating. . . . Our job . . . is put forth by the Bible."

But Topeka West High had a problem with Sam's "community service." It wasn't exactly what they had in mind when they told the kids to go out and do good works. So they informed Sam he'd be receiving "no extra credit."

Sam's grandfather, the Reverend Fred, who's running for the U.S. Senate from Kansas, didn't like that. The school district was afraid he would sue them. Meanwhile, the mayor of Topeka gave Sam his own community service award. Eventually, the school system backed down. They compromised with Sam, saying they'd give him the extra credit, but that they would have to put down that it was for baby-sitting and other things. That was okay with Sam, and so he got his extra credit.

I started to wonder—if you can get extra credit in Topeka for bashing gays and people with AIDS, what else might school authorities consider to help improve students' grades?

I decided to submit the following list of extra-credit courses to the principal of Topeka West. These should all qualify as "good deeds" along the lines of what Sam Phelps was recognized for. Here's how these classes should be listed in the course handbook.

101. EXTRA CREDIT IN GRAPHIC DESIGN

Students will go on field trips to the local abortion clinic and take photos of women going in for an abortion. They will bring them back to class and lay them out on poster-size paper under the heading THIS WOMAN KILLED HER BABY. The school print shop will then take the layout and run off hundreds of handbills. Students who post them around town will also receive credit.

204. EXTRA CREDIT FOR BIOLOGY AND/OR PHYSICS

Did you know there are other uses for fertilizer than spreading it around cow pastures? Learn ways to harness the incredible, amazing energy and force of fertilizer with helpful lads from the local army base near Junction City, Kansas. (Students must pay for own fuses.)

303. EXTRA CREDIT IN HEALTH

Help say no to drugs! If your parents smoke pot, this class will help you turn them in to the authorities. Also, you will be taught the techniques of police entrapment and receive hands-on experience by "selling" drugs in school and apprehending your fellow classmates.

409. EXTRA CREDIT IN HOME ECONOMICS

The local order of the National Association for the Advancement of White People needs their sheets cleaned and pressed every Saturday morning. Students can also claim credit for Social Studies.

502. EXTRA CREDIT IN INTERNATIONAL AFFAIRS

Our local immigration authorities have their hands full with all the illegals coming into our area. This is your chance to learn about the world around you. For every *hombre* you spot, we'll raise your grade a half point. For each one you apprehend, a full point. Take 'em out with a single shot, and you're in the National Honor Society!

• • •

After waiting for over a month to see if the principal of Topeka West would take my suggestions, we decided to give him a call. He said that he would not be offering any of my extra-credit classes.

That's what's wrong with our educational system—principals who don't see the merit of rewarding *all* forms of bigotry.

Take That Pen
Out of
Bob Dole's Hand

THERE THEY WERE, twenty feet from me, walking through the door, virtually hand in hand. Bob Dole and Newt Gingrich, the Conservative Couplet. I was attending a meeting of the Republican governors in 1995, not because I was a Republican governor, but because I was attempting to set a record by becoming the first American man to have hugged all fifty governors. I know it sounds a little crazy but, dammit, Congress was returning power to the states, so I personally wanted to *touch* that power like no man had ever touched it before.

About a dozen of the Republican governors had already reluctantly (but tenderly) given me a hug when, without warning, in through the door walked

CHAPTER 30

Dole *and* Gingrich. (They weren't Republican governors, either, and I didn't notice them doing any hugging, so why the hell were they there?)

Their reactions to seeing me couldn't have been more different from each other. Gingrich immediately instructed security to surround him so that I could not get near him. There was this sick look on his face. Have you seen that look people have when Ed McMahon appears at their door with the $10 million check? Not that look.

Newt's face twisted into the sort of revulsion you reserve for occasions when you bump into a guy you realize is peeing on the sidewalk. It was a look I had sadly witnessed before on the faces of others who had seen *Roger & Me*, and wished to avoid the "me" of that movie. The rejection always hurts, and I feel like blurting out, "Please don't run away— I'm an Eagle Scout!"

Gingrich and his bodyguards, in a tight formation, moved quickly by me before I could explain that I didn't want to hug *him*.

Dole, though, when he spotted me, flashed a big grin across his face, gave a little wave as he came toward me, and mouthed "Hi, Mike!" with his lips. It did not matter to him that I aspired to be a poster boy for every cause he opposed. No, the equation, for Bob Dole, was quite simple: I appeared to be of voting age, and that meant only one thing—Fresh Meat! I was a potential Bob Dole voter! Also, I had a TV crew with me, which, in turn, meant reaching more Potential Bob Dole Voters. That's all that counts when your only career is getting elected.

I held out my hand to shake his, and as I went to reach for his right hand, he pulled it back. Jeez, I thought, I'm not going to steal that pen you're holding . . . and then, like a dope, I remembered: *he can't shake my hand the "normal" way*. I felt so embarrassed. There was his right hand, ravaged from a war wound, with a ballpoint pen sticking out of it. I had forgotten about the war wound. He held out his left hand and I shook it. Before I could say anything, he uttered a "glad to see you here," kept his smile frozen, and then was on to the next Potential Bob Dole Voter.

I was bothered by this for some time, not knowing how to come to grips with Dole's right hand. He did a brave thing in 1943 when he crawled out of his foxhole to save his radioman, who had been hit by German gunfire. Dole was then shot himself, and the wounds were so grievous the medics decided he was near death in their triage of the battleground. They marked him with a big *M* on his forehead (they used his own blood), meaning they'd already given him as much morphine as possible, and moved on to others who stood a better chance of living.

But Bob Dole was far from dead and gone. He lived, and though he was paralyzed from the neck down, after three years of rehabilitation and operations, everything was back to normal except his right hand and arm.

That's a great story, and one to be proud of. And Dole has no problem retelling it. But he's not proud of his damaged right hand, and seems to have found it to be an embarrassment. So one day he got the bright idea of sticking a pen in his hand, making it look as if he were always about ready to sign some important document. But the pen was there only as an ornament in order to mask the "ugliness" of his hand.

It is this kind of attitude that has kept handicapped people "out of sight, out of mind" all these years. We did not want to look at their deformities, so we called them "shut-ins" and kept them out of the workplace, out of the theaters and restaurants, off the sidewalks, and out of the public eye. It was more comfortable for us that way.

But thanks to disabled rights activists, laws were written to stop this kind of discrimination. Curbs were cut. Ramps built. Elevators installed. The idea is that we should look at people who have physical differences as being as normal as you or I, even if it means giving them more spaces than seemingly necessary near the entrance of the mall and making us walk a half a mile to get to the J. C. Penney's.

So, just as we were starting to get over our hang-ups regarding the disabled, along comes Bob Dole and his pen.

I would like to say this to Mr. Dole: TAKE THAT DAMN PEN OUT OF YOUR HAND! There is nothing wrong with your hand, it looks just fine, we will not hold its deformity against you. We are all proud of what you did for this country.

Yes, I understand old habits are hard to break, and who am I to tell you what to do about something that obviously bothers you a great deal. So you need to hold a prop. Fine. But a *pen?* C'mon, Bob, I don't think so. Do you feel that it makes you look like a statesman? The pen is the tool of a writer, which you are not. The pen is used by the President to sign bills into law, which you really shouldn't plan on doing.

The pen, Bob, is all wrong. You need to be holding on to something that is more appropriate for the man you are. You need to be grabbing on to an object that symbolizes the kind of congressman and senator you've been for the past thirty-six years in Washington, D.C.

If you absolutely feel you must be holding something in that hand, may I suggest a few other items that say, definitively, *"THIS IS BOB DOLE!"* so much better than a twenty-nine-cent Bic?

Take a look at how great you'd come across with any of these devices in your hand:

MR. DOLE, YOU have been a leader in the movement to repeal the ban on assault weapons in this country. You believe that, after a quick "computer check," *anyone* should be able to buy assault weapons. This is comforting news to Americans, especially parents who live in our large urban centers.

Think of it, Bob—everywhere you go, you have that Uzi in your hand! You would not only look tough and macho, you would be making an important political statement: Easy Guns for Everyone!

BOB, YOU WANT to overturn the Supreme Court's *Roe v. Wade* decision, which made abortion legal. You want a constitutional amendment banning all abortions except in cases of rape or incest, or where giving birth threatens the life of the mother. At different times lately you have agreed with one, two, or none of these exemptions. (Note: You need only one position on this matter.)

If you succeed in outlawing abortion, that would return us to the good old dirty, unsafe days when thousands of women were injured or died as a result of "doctors" using everything from coat hangers to sulfuric acid to terminate pregnancies.

Nothing will make the Buchanan supporters and the Christian Coalition happier than to see you marching down Pennsylvania Avenue on Inauguration Day with a big ol' coat hanger stuck in your right hand!

SINCE 1973, BOB, you have raised over $70 million in special interest money, more than anyone else running for president in 1996. You are completely bought by, and beholden to, Big Business in this country.

I guess when your parents moved you and your siblings out of the upstairs and into the basement so they could rent out the main part of your house to make a few extra dollars during the Depression, you decided right then and there you were never going to be in that cellar again.

And speaking of cellars, what better company to have as your number one contributor than Ernest and Julio Gallo, the wine kings! They've contributed over $1 million to your campaigns and your foundation. In return for their generosity, you got legislation passed exempting Gallo from a part of the tax code that saved them over $100 million in inheritance taxes! Salut, Bob! Carry that bottle with pride.

Free Us, Nelson Mandela!

FROM 1948 TO 1991, the black citizens of South Africa endured a system known as apartheid. It was legalized segregation, and it codified a strict set of rules that set up two societies, one white and one black. Blacks were kept in their place by this system, never able to hold power or wealth, even though they made up 75 percent of the population.

CHAPTER 31

But then along came a man named Nelson Mandela, who became a leader of the African National Congress. Their fight against apartheid resulted in Mandela spending over twenty-seven years in jail.

During his last ten years in prison, a group of Americans, led by Randall Robinson and others, began a campaign in this country to persuade the U.S. government and corporations to end their support of South Africa. Twenty-seven states and almost a hundred cities passed divestment ordinances affecting $25 to $30 billion worth of stock in companies doing business with South Africa. College students protested by constructing shantytowns on their campuses. Celebrities and members of Congress committed acts of civil disobedience by getting arrested at the South African embassy in D.C.

The result of all of this was one of the few great successes the Left has enjoyed in my lifetime—an end to South African apartheid! The campaign worked. Relentless mass political action with a blow below the economic belt actually brought about a historic change.

But today there is another country where blacks are forced to live primarily in ghetto "townships," where crime and lawlessness are rampant and the police abuse the residents at will. A country where blacks occupy most of the unskilled, low-paying jobs while whites sit in corner suites of office high-rises. A country where black babies have a greater chance of dying than babies born in the poorest slums of the Third World. A country where black children go to schools that are more like prisons, while the white children work away on their IBMs in clean, safe environments.

That country, of course, is the United States. And thus I am hoping to persuade Nelson Mandela to help us lead a new movement—against *American* apartheid. "FREE *US*, MR. MANDELA!"

This would not be an easy task. Apartheid in the United States is not so brazen; it doesn't appear on our law books. In fact, unlike the old South Africa, blacks in the United States can and do vote, hold office, own property, marry the person of their choice, attend universities, and have available to them legal protections if they are discriminated against.

So what's the big deal?

Here's the big deal:

We continue to have a major problem with race in America, no matter how much we want to believe otherwise. Whites insist that things have gotten better. Look at all the black congressmen! Look at the new black middle class! Look at Martin Lawrence—he's got his own show! Many whites complain that affirmative action has gone too far. "If only I were black, I woulda got the job." If I had a dollar for every time I've heard that line, I wouldn't need a job.

According to *The New York Times,* some states, like Pennsylvania and Arizona, are trying to outlaw affirmative action. In more than a dozen states, such as South Carolina and Washington, movements are under way to amend the state constitution or put initiatives on the ballot to outlaw affirmative action. The university systems in California, Colorado, and Texas have rescinded certain affirmative action programs. When the new Republican governor of Louisiana, Mike Foster, took over in 1995, his first executive order reversed all of the state's affirmative action programs. And legislation to outlaw affirmative action at the federal level, called the Equal Opportunity Act of 1996, is now moving through Congress.

To those whites who feel we've gone too far with civil rights, and that blacks have "got it made," let me ask you this question: Would you, right now, willingly trade places with a black man or woman living in America? Are you really saying to me, "Gee, I wish I were black! Life would be so much better! I'd climb the ladder to the top! Imagine my opportunities—live in a big house wherever I want, freely walk at night on any suburban street, attend the best private colleges, and the best jobs are mine for the picking! Oh, please, God, make me black, black, BLACK!"

I don't think so.

We have stuck our heads in the sand so long, we can't see just how bad American apartheid has become. Why are white people surprised when Black America stands and cheers the O.J. verdict?

We are, in a word, clueless.

But Black America isn't. Consider this:

- Black infants are twice as likely as white infants to die in the first year of life.

- For every dollar earned by white men, black men earn 74 cents and black women 64 cents. The typical white person's net worth is ten times that of blacks. Sixty-seven percent of black families do not make the country's average family income. The average white family has an annual income of $39,000 a year; the average black family is paid $21,550.

- Forty-nine mortgage lenders in sixteen big cities studied by Ralph Nader's office engage in racial redlining, a practice where banks and other lenders avoid making loans in minority neighborhoods. The sixteen cities are Boston, New York, Buffalo, Philadelphia, Pittsburgh, Baltimore, Washington, Atlanta, Miami, Chicago, Detroit, St. Louis, Dallas, Houston, Los Angeles, and Oakland.

- The Baton Rouge, Louisiana, school board released a draft report in March 1996 indicating that black students perform below white students in all 42 possible comparisons on the Louisiana Educational Assessment Program tests.

- In 1994, nearly one in three black males in their twenties were in prison, on parole, or otherwise under the supervision of the criminal justice system.

Who better to liberate us from our system of American Apartheid than Nelson Mandela!

I placed a call to the South African consulate in New York

to make my request. I was greeted at first with some confusion, but the vice-consul said she understood what I was getting at. Unfortunately, she told me, the South African government does not interfere in the affairs of another country. I told her, had that been our attitude in the 1980s, apartheid in South Africa might never have ended.

It then struck me that we were, in part, responsible for South Africa's apartheid conditions and therefore had a moral responsibility to help eradicate it. I felt a little embarrassed, so I thanked her and wished her well.

"But feel free to make a request to President Mandela," she interjected as I began to hang up. "You never know what he may be able to do to help."

Next, I called Randall Robinson's group, TransAfrica, to see if they would help me free Black America like they helped to free Black South Africa.

I was told by information specialist Mwiza Munthali that U.S. domestic issues do not fall under the mission of TransAfrica, but good luck.

Well, I didn't get very far. So, for those of you who want to join me in this anti–American Apartheid campaign, here's what I propose we do:

1. Demand that our universities divest themselves of corporations whose boards of directors are 100 percent white, which include the following (as of summer 1996): American International Group (insurance company); American Brands (Benson & Hedges cigarettes, Jim Beam bourbon); Archer Daniels Midland; Becton, Dickinson and Co. (medical supplies and diagnostic equipment); Burlington Resources (oil and gas producer); Cabletron Systems (computer network systems manufacturer); Chris-Craft (yacht maker); Church & Dwight Co. (Arm & Hammer baking soda); H. J. Heinz; Ingersoll-Rand (machine tools, construction, and mining equipment); Illinois Tool Works; James River Corporation of Virginia (Dixie paper cups); Microsoft;

Mylan Labs (generic drugs); Reynolds Metals; J. M. Smucker; Safeway; and Sherwin-Williams.

2. Encourage college students to begin setting up mock tenement buildings on their campuses and refuse to take them down until banks change their discriminatory lending practices. I want to see a cardboard version of the Brewster Housing Project right smack in the middle of the diag in Ann Arbor.

3. Get Kweisi Mfume (the new head of the NAACP) and Bella Abzug to hold daily civil disobedience protests in front of the New York Stock Exchange. Encourage foreign countries to hold similar protests in front of U.S. embassies and U.S. corporate headquarters abroad. Do not stop the civil disobedience until Corporate America levels out the economic playing field.

4. Demand a release of the tens of thousands of black inmates in U.S. prisons who are there for nonviolent crimes. Give each of these newly released inmates a good-paying job. The U.S. has now surpassed South Africa as the country with the largest prison population in the world. This should be an embarrassment.

This anti–American Apartheid movement may be a bit more difficult than the one against South Africa, but if Nelson Mandela will return my call, I believe, in my heart of hearts, he'll be able to help us out of the mess we're in.

NAFTA's Great! Let's Move Washington to Tijuana!

IN 1994, THE North American Free Trade Agreement took effect. No other single government document has done more to downsize this country than NAFTA. More and more jobs are exported every day from the United States into Mexico, with over 60,000 laid-off workers in the U.S. having already qualified for federal benefits. There are now 20 percent more employees in U.S. companies operating in Mexico than before NAFTA went into effect. It is no coincidence that the number one employer in Mexico today is our number one downsizing leader, General Motors.

CHAPTER 32

NAFTA was supported by a diverse coalition of businesses, industry front groups, and industry-financed politicians from Bill Clinton to Bob Dole.

They all claimed that the three-way deal between Canada, Mexico, and the United States would boost U.S. exports and lead to higher wages. They were right. The executives' wages have skyrocketed to an all-time high.

Sly politicos like Pat Buchanan and Ross Perot have tried to seize NAFTA and make some hay of their own. What Pat and Ross don't understand is just what a great idea NAFTA is.

In fact, I believe that if our leaders in Congress and the White House are so convinced that NAFTA will create jobs, cut expenses, and save money, then I can think of just one thing for them to do:

Try it out for themselves! Let's move D.C. to Tijuana!

Why not? If it's good enough for General Motors, it should be good enough for Congress. The taxpayers want a smaller federal government. What better way to shrink it than by moving it to Mexico?

And the federal government has made it easier than ever before, thanks to their own Department of Commerce's NAFTA office, which helps industry navigate through (and around) labor, immigration, and trade laws while doing business in Mexico.

Imagine . . . instead of paying high-priced staffers to do their fetching, the House and Senate can hire those border kids selling Chiclets! The Pentagon would no longer have to pay for the upkeep of the world's largest office building— they could build a replica for pennies on the dollar in Acapulco! And what about the Vice President's office and mansion? Who the hell would miss it? Move it to the Yucatán!

I can think of no better person to head up this move than Lawrence Bossidy, CEO of Allied Signal. He has led the way by example—exporting jobs to Mexico from at least five different U.S. cities: El Paso, Texas; Orangeburg, South Carolina; Greenville, Alabama; Eatontown, New Jersey; and Greenville, Ohio. With compensation of $12.4 million a year, Bossidy earned more than the combined annual wages of his 3,800-person workforce in Monterrey, Mexico. Imagine the size of next year's bonus package when he helps to shift the entire U.S. government to Mexico!

I propose that the first federal department to make the move should be the headquarters of NAFTA itself—the Department of Commerce! No one seems to like this agency to begin with. The captains of commerce don't want some Commerce Department telling them how to do business. Although they tempered their criticism of the department shortly after the death of its Secretary, Ron Brown, Republican leaders seemed over their grief in about three weeks when they publicly called for the dismantling of Commerce.

What surprises me is that these Republicans have overlooked this obvious solution to what they believe is a bloated agency. Moving it to Mexico would save millions of federal dollars *and* showcase the Department of Commerce's best success, NAFTA. Think of all the good reasons to move the Commerce Department to Mexico:

1. A Huge Savings. First and foremost, it would save us taxpayers bundles of money. Wages for salaried and hourly employees are one of the biggest outlays in the department's budget—over $1.6 billion. Qualified Mexicans can do the *same* job for a *fraction* of the cost. Also, the main Commerce building is located in the heart of our nation's capital. That's prime real estate. Think of the revenue those one million square feet on Pennsylvania Avenue will generate for Uncle Sam in rentals!

2. Do As I Say, Do As I Do. Moving the Commerce Department to Mexico would set a good example for employers across the nation and send a clear signal to all Americans that Commerce means business. People are always complaining that the federal government is all talk and no action, that it operates with a double standard. What better way to talk the talk and walk the walk with NAFTA than to move the cabinet-level agency responsible for it south of the border?

3. Easy Access. Logistically, it makes sense for the Commerce Department to operate in full force in Mexico, since so many thousands of American businesses will be operating there. The International Trade Administration, Bureau of Export Administration, and Office of Tourism Industries should be nowhere else but in downtown Tijuana!

This idea may not be popular at first within the Commerce Department itself. That is understandable. Approximately 19,000 D.C.-based employees stand to lose their jobs if this move goes through. But President Clinton loves to quote from a new national study that says more than one-quarter of all laid-off workers find new jobs that pay at least as much as their old jobs. So Commerce employees should look on the bright side! And the other three-quarters who may never find comparable-paying, full-time work won't lose out entirely; if they ever earn an income again, they will end up paying less in taxes thanks to the savings of moving the federal government to Mexico. I am confident those savings will trickle down to them through tax cuts.

And here's the best part: while they are out of work, Commerce employees can qualify for seventy-eight weeks of state and federal unemployment benefits (sometimes up to half their old paychecks!) and up to two years of federally funded retraining (which could include Spanish language classes to prepare them for the workplace of the future).

Since Mickey Kantor, the man who negotiated NAFTA for the Clinton administration, is now the Secretary of Commerce, this move would be a sign of goodwill on his part.

Hopefully, his twenty-three undersecretaries and assistant secretaries and his 218 political appointees will get on the bandwagon and sell this move to their employees and the nation. No doubt most of them would prefer a tropical climate to a swamp.

Congress was on recess when I first had this idea, so I decided to take it upon myself to jump-start the move. First, I called the Commerce Department itself and spoke with someone in the NAFTA office at the International Trade Administration. I told her I had an operation in mind that I would like to be moved to Mexico. She was very accommodating. She faxed to me, free of charge, U.S. government–printed fact sheets, phone lists, and other resources to help me get the ball rolling, including:

- U.S. Department of Commerce NAFTA Facts Document 8106: a list of Mexican publications for advertising jobs.

- Document 8308: information about Mexican immigration procedures for intercompany transferees.

- Document 8502: a guide to Mexican compensation and labor law.

- Document 8203: a list of chambers of commerce and trade commissions that help U.S. businesses conduct operations in Mexico.

- Document 8113: a business fact sheet on Mexico.

Using these guides prepared by our very own Commerce Department, I took out classified ads in newspapers in the border towns of Nuevo Laredo, Piedras Negras, Reynosa, Ciudad Juárez, and Tijuana to see whether qualified workers were available and interested in applying for a job with the U.S. Commerce Department.

Here's how the ad read:

I received hundreds of replies from Mexicans desperate to work for Americans.

Next, I made discreet inquiries with realtors in those same border areas about renting or purchasing approximately one million square feet of office space. I discovered that prices for buildings within five hundred meters of the border (easy access for those assistant secretaries and undersecretaries who wish to live in U.S. border towns and make the daily commute to Mexico) range from twenty-five to thirty-one pesos (three to four dollars) per square meter, depending on the site and the amenities. Although it may be difficult to acquire one facility with one million square feet of space, I have five realtors throughout the border areas on the lookout.

I called the U.S. embassy in Mexico City and spoke with Angeles Avila, a U.S. trade specialist in the embassy's Commercial Service division, and explained to her that I wanted to move offices to Mexico to save on labor costs. She was very encouraging and faxed me thirteen pages of real estate contacts, human resources and personnel recruiting contacts, and registration forms for establishing a foreign company in Mexico—all compliments of the American government. Angeles also gave me the phone number of Manpower Mexico, the temporary employment agency.

Perla Galarza of Manpower Mexico was eager to arrange to supply hundreds of bilingual clerical and secretarial workers ("with pretty good, but not perfect, English") at a cost of $3.73 per hour. Compare this to federal-sector secretaries in the United States, who earn between ten and fifteen dollars per hour plus benefits. A year's worth of savings on payroll costs alone will more than pay for the move.

So in less than a week, I laid the groundwork to move the U.S. Department of Commerce to any one of five Mexican border towns. The hard part was over.

It is now up to the Congress and the President to take the next step. And if the legislative or executive branches get cold feet, here's one last suggestion: use the *threat* of a move and massive layoffs to force the employees of Commerce to accept a 20 percent across-the-board wage cut.

That little practical joke *always* works in the private sector. *Hasta luego, El Commercia!*

Why Doesn't GM Sell Crack?

PEOPLE IN THE business world like to say, "Profit is supreme." They like chanting that.

"Profit is king." That's another one they like to repeat. They don't like to say, "I'll pick up the check." That means less profit. Profit is what it's all about. When they say "the bottom line," they mean their *profit*. They like that bottom line to contain a number followed by a lot of zeroes.

If I had a nickel for every time I heard some guy in a suit tell me that "a company must do whatever is necessary to create the biggest profit possible," I would have a very big bottom line right now. Here's another popular mantra: "The responsibility of the CEO is to make his shareholders as much money as he can."

CHAPTER 33

Are you enjoying this lesson in capitalism? I get it every time I fly on a plane. The bottom-line feeders have all seen *Roger & Me,* yet they often mistake the fuselage of a DC-9 for the Oxford Debating Society. So I have to sit through lectures ad nauseam about the beauties of our free market system. Today the guy in the seat next to me is the owner of an American company that makes office supplies—in Taiwan. I ask the executive, "How much is 'enough'?"

"Enough what?" he replies.

"How much is 'enough' profit?"

He laughs and says, "There's no such thing as 'enough'!"

"So, General Motors made nearly $7 billion in profit last year—but they could make $7.*1* billion by closing a factory in Parma, Ohio, and moving it to Mexico—that would be okay?"

"Not only okay," he responds, "it is their duty to close that plant and make the extra $.1 billion."

"Even if it destroys Parma, Ohio? Why can't $7 billion be enough and spare the community? Why ruin thousands of families for the sake of *$.1* billion? Do you think this is *moral?*"

"Moral?" he asks, as if this is the first time he's heard that word since First Communion class. "This is not an issue of morality. It is purely a matter of economics. A company must be able to do whatever it wants to make a profit." Then he leans over as if to make a revelation I've never heard before.

"Profit, you know, is supreme."

So here's what I don't understand: if profit is supreme, why doesn't a company like General Motors sell crack? Crack is a *very* profitable commodity. For every pound of cocaine that is transformed into crack, a dealer stands to make a profit of $45,000. The dealer profit on a two-thousand-pound car is less than $2,000. Crack is also safer to use than automobiles. Each year, 40,000 people die in car accidents. Crack, on the other hand, kills only a few hundred people a year. And it doesn't pollute.

So why doesn't GM sell crack? If profit is supreme, why not sell crack?

GM doesn't sell crack because it is illegal. Why is it illegal? Because we, as a society, have determined that crack destroys people's lives. It ruins entire communities. It tears apart the very backbone of our country. That's why we wouldn't let a company like GM sell it, no matter what kind of profit they could make.

If we wouldn't let GM sell crack because it destroys our communities, then why do we let them close factories? *That, too,* destroys our communities.

As my frequent-flier friend would say, "We can't prevent them from closing factories because they have a right to do whatever they want to in order to make a profit."

No, they don't. They don't have a "right" to do a lot of things: sell child pornography, manufacture chemical weapons, or create hazardous products that could conceivably make them a profit. We can enact laws to prevent companies from doing anything to hurt us.

And downsizing is one of those things that is hurting us. I'm not talking about legitimate layoffs, when a company is losing money and simply doesn't have the cash reserves to pay its workers. I'm talking about companies like GM, AT&T, and GE, which fire people at a time when the company is making record profits in the billions of dollars. Executives who do this are not scorned, picketed, or arrested—they are hailed as heroes! They make the covers of *Fortune* and *Forbes.* They lecture at the Harvard Business School about their success. They throw big campaign fund-raisers and sit next to the President of the United States. They are the Masters of the Universe simply because they make huge profits regardless of the consequences to our society.

Are we insane or what? Why do we allow this to happen? It is *wrong* to make money off people's labor and then fire them after you've made it. It is *immoral* for a CEO to make millions of dollars when he has just destroyed the livelihood of 40,000 families. And it's just plain *nuts* to allow American companies to move factories overseas at the expense of our own people.

When a company fires thousands of people, what happens to the community? Crime goes up, suicide goes up, drug abuse, alcoholism, spousal abuse, divorce—everything bad spirals dangerously upward. The same thing happens with crack. Only crack is illegal, and downsizing is not. If there was a crack house in your neighborhood, what would you do? You would try to get rid of it!

I think it's time we applied the same attitudes we have about crack to corporate downsizing. It's simple: if it hurts our citizens, it should be illegal. We live in a democracy. We enact laws based on what we believe is right and wrong. Murder? Wrong, so we pass a law making it illegal. Burglary? Wrong, and we attempt to prosecute those who commit it. Two really big hairy guys from Gingrich's office pummel me after they read this book? Five to ten in Sing Sing.

As a society, we have a right to protect ourselves from harm. As a democracy, we have a responsibility to legislate measures to protect us from harm.

Here's what I think we should do to protect ourselves:

1. Prohibit corporations from closing a profitable factory or business and moving it overseas. If they close a business and move it within the U.S., they must pay reparations to the community they are leaving behind. We've passed divorce laws that say that if a woman works hard to put her husband through school, and he later decides to leave her after he has become successful, he has a responsibility to compensate her for her sacrifices that allowed him to go on to acquire his wealth. The "marriage" between a company and a community should be no different. If a corporation packs up and leaves, it should have some serious alimony to pay.

2. Prohibit companies from pitting one state or city against another. We are all Americans. It is no victory for our society when one town wins at another's expense. Texas should not be able to raid Massachusetts for jobs. It is debilitating and, frankly, legal extortion.

3. Institute a 100 percent tax on any profits gained by shareholders when the company's stock goes up due to an announcement of firings. No one should be allowed to profit from such bad news.

4. Prohibit executives' salaries from being more than thirty times greater than an average employee's pay. When workers have to take a wage cut because of hard times, so, too, should the CEO. If a CEO fires a large number of employees, it should be illegal for him to collect a bonus that year.

5. Require boards of directors of publicly owned corporations to have representation from both workers and consumers. A company will run better if it has to listen to the people who have to build and/or use the products the company makes.

For those of you free-marketers who disagree with these modest suggestions and may end up on a plane sitting next to me, screaming, "You can't tell a business how it can operate!"—I have this to say: Oh, yes, we can! We legally require companies to build safe products, to ensure safe workplaces, to pay employees a minimum wage, to contribute to their Social Security, and to follow a host of other rules that we, as a society, have deemed necessary for our well-being. And we can legally require each of the steps I've outlined above.

GM can't sell crack. Soon, I predict, they and other companies will not be able to sell us out. Just keep firing more workers, my friends, and see what happens.

I Want My Tax Break
or I'm Leaving

The Hon. Rudolph Giuliani
Mayor of New York City
City Hall
61 Chambers Street
New York, New York 10007

Dear Mr. Mayor:

I have noticed that the city has been handing out a lot of tax breaks recently. You've said you needed to do this in order to keep corporations in the city. You said that they would move to New Jersey if you didn't cough up the money.

I understand your concern. We need to keep jobs in New York. Not to mention the tax base. Somebody's gotta pay for George Steinbrenner!

That is why I am writing to you. I believe my presence in the city is also valuable—maybe even more valuable than First Boston, to whom you gave a $50 million tax break. And *then* they cut nine hundred jobs—something I would *never* do if you found it in your heart to slide a little of the joy—and free money—my way.

Let me explain.

Since coming to New York a few years ago, I have paid over $30,000 in taxes to the city. That is enough to pay the annual salary of your groundskeeper at Gracie Mansion. I know you like your groundskeeper, and I would hate for you to lose him if I were to leave the city.

Please note, I only said "if." This is in no way, shape, or form a "threat" on my part. I LOVE NY! Have you ever been to Flint, Michigan? You'd LOVE NY, too!

My presence in the city has also brought untold employment to hundreds of individuals, including video store clerks, subway conductors, lawyers at Warner Bros., cable guys, Chinese food deliverers, lawyers at NBC, movie theater ticket takers, the booker on Conan O'Brien, meter maids, lawyers at Fox, bartenders, network censors, clerks at Tower Records, the priest at Holy Trinity, lawyers at Random House, the kid who waters our plants when we're gone, and the Soup Nazi.

As you can see, I have been responsible for a significant number of jobs here in the past few years. And this doesn't even count the people who keep sending me notices for jury duty! My vacating the city would have a serious and dire impact on all of the above-named individuals. Placing them on the public dole will only strain your resources further.

Did I say "vacating"? Please forgive me! Banish the thought from your head! I would hate to think it would ever come to that!

Aside from the obvious tax and employment advantages of keeping me in New York ("Keeping?" Where else would I go?!), I believe there are other reasons I am the type of citizen you want. I obey all the laws, don't pollute the Hudson (I ship my garbage to Orange County, CA!), don't own a car (no congestion!), and am a generous patron of the arts, mostly at your fine karaoke bars.

Thank you for taking the time to consider my request. A 50 percent tax abatement for the next twenty years would go a long way toward persuading me not to take all of these jobs and revenues back to my home state of Michigan (ugh!), where the people are in desperate need of my largesse.

Yours truly,

Michael Moore

• • •

The Hon. Woodrow Stanley
Mayor of the City of Flint
City Hall
South Saginaw Street
Flint, Michigan 48502

Dear Mr. Mayor:

Although it's been some time since we chatted—and I understand from mutual acquaintances that you are still peeved about *Roger & Me*—I believe I have an offer you cannot refuse.

Over the past eighteen years you have personally voted for every tax break General Motors has asked you for. In all, over $1.8 billion worth of property has received tax abatements, allowing GM to avoid paying taxes on up to 50 percent of this property for up to twelve years.

As a result of this generosity on your part, the city and the school district have been left short of cash—a *lot* of cash. This has caused a cutback in city services (remember when garbage could only be picked up once every *two* weeks—P.U.!) and has forced schools to close. It must upset you that during that time GM didn't create a single new job—and it was certainly big of you not to ask for your gift (the tax breaks) back from them.

But you are obviously in need of some dinero. So I have a proposal. Why don't you give me a 100 percent tax break—and I'll move all of my production back to Flint!

That's right—movies, television, publishing—hell, I'll bring the damn Ice Capades there! Imagine, Flint, Michigan—ENTERTAINMENT CAPITAL OF THE MIDWEST!

I hear you're thinking of tearing down the old, boarded-up AutoWorld theme park—that big, beautiful homage to the auto industry that you and the other council members helped to build in order to bring a million tourists a year to Flint. There's no reason to destroy the place when *we* could just move in there—rent-free, of course. We could call it "MikeWorld"! Forget about Hollywood and Vine—all of America will be rushing to MikeWorld to be on TV or in the movies!

All of this will increase the tax base, provide employment, fill up the empty hotels with tourists, and save your butt in the next election! You can't go wrong!

Woody, deliver me from this awful city of New York! You can't get a decent burger here for less than ten dollars!

Yours in solidarity,

Mike

Michael Moore

Mike's Militia

ARE YOU FEELING just a little left out of the militia movement? It seems like everybody's got a militia these days.

Running around in the woods, firing guns, always on the lookout for black helicopters carrying secret agents of the federal government—or worse, the United Nations! Sounds cool, huh? But they're so damn nuts! And hairy. Big hairy guys with beer guts carrying guns is not my idea of fun.

CHAPTER 35

So I've decided to create an alternative for those of us who are still pretty pissed off but don't want to overthrow the United States government and replace it with big hairy guys. I am forming a militia I can call my own—Mike's Militia—a sort of all-purpose group for the firearm-challenged. There are no dues in Mike's Militia, no meetings, and no letterhead. The purpose of Mike's Militia is threefold:

1. To enforce the calls to action in this book, from protecting a sperm's right to life to helping law enforcement officials apprehend any and all corporate welfare mothers and criminals.
2. To sell raffle tickets (First Prize: a cruise with Kathie Lee Gifford; Second Prize: dinner with Newt's first wife). The proceeds will be used for militia members to go on really cool field trips to places like the Nixon Library and John du Pont's World of Wrestling, play 18 holes with O.J. and his Abusive Men's Support Group, or hold a sleepover in the Unabomber's shack.
3. To eliminate all other militia groups.

With my militia all set to go, I went to meet the grand-daddy of militia leaders, Commander Norman Olson, cofounder of the Michigan Militia.

That's Norm Olson sitting next to me in the photo (preceding page). We're on the Ferris wheel singing "If I Had a Hammer." A few days after the Oklahoma City bombing, Norm came to national prominence when it was revealed that Timothy McVeigh and Terry Nichols had attended meetings of his Michigan Militia prior to the bombing. McVeigh and Nichols were living northeast of Flint on a farm where they practiced their bomb-making in the back-yard. Suddenly, Commander Olson was in demand. That's why I had to see him.

I met him at his home in northern Michigan where he greeted me at the door with an AK-47, proving he had a sense of humor along with an instinct to kill jerks like me. Norm and his men had been conducting maneuvers in the woods nearby with their guns and camouflage and had just taken a well-deserved break.

I asked Norm if he would put down his guns and join Mike's Militia.

"What's Mike's Militia?" he wanted to know.

"You'll see," I told him. "Just trust me."

Amazingly, Norm and his men agreed to join my militia—for at least one day. I then put them through a series of grueling maneuvers. Our field log read as follows:

- 2:05 P.M.: Attended the local Catholic carnival. Rode the Tilt-a-Whirl and the Ferris wheel while singing "Kumbaya" and the Carpenters' 1971 hit, "For All We Know." Knights of Columbus officials asked us to leave.
- 3:12 P.M.: Drove in single-line formation to the local root beer stand. Ate burgers and fries. Norm ordered seconds.

- 5:01 P.M.: Everyone was given KP duty. Baked a cake together in Norm's kitchen. Norm insisted on decorating the cake with an American flag and a cross in red dye #2 icing.
- 7:33 P.M.: Shore duty on Lake Michigan. Skipped stones on the lake.
- 8:55 P.M.: Read some of Norm's poetry aloud on the pier while Mike strummed a guitar.

Norm and the boys did pretty well with my training, considering none of them could carry a tune. We had a great time, and soon I could see they were starting to melt. Norm told me how he, too, had grown up in the Flint area, as did his wife, who went to high school in the district next to mine. One of Norm's men said he had gone to my wife's high school. We all had come from the same place, with similar beginnings to our lives. Yet we had obviously taken different roads.

By day's end, Norm and the boys were getting tired. I asked them to take an oath forsaking violence. Norm told me he didn't expect to be alive a year from now, that the final confrontation with the government was coming and he would probably die defending his beliefs. I gave him a swig of my Snapple and wished him well. He asked me one final question.

"You know, you guys were right in the sixties," Norm said. "The government lied to us. They probably killed Dr. King. Us conservatives were wrong. So when we finally wised up in the nineties, after all these jobs were lost, where were you liberals when we needed your help?"

I didn't have an answer. Where *were* the liberals, the Democrats, the lefties, the feminists, the peaceniks? Why weren't we there for the Norman Olsons when, at the moment the American Dream was ripped from him and his friends, they needed some answers, some direction? Too busy meeting with ourselves, I guess.

Remember Mark from Michigan? He surfaced after the Oklahoma bombing with his infamous radio broadcasts and faxes to congressmen and the NRA. But get this: he's a janitor at one of the most liberal schools in America, the University of Michigan in Ann Arbor! What is the Left in Ann Arbor doing while Mark from Michigan is scrubbing their floors and toilets? I can just see it now—all the groovy nineties lefties holding their PC meetings in Room 305 of the student union, talking about the oppressed masses and not even noticing the oppressed Mark from Michigan who has to pick up their half-empty Starbucks cups filled with soaked cigarette butts. Mark needs some help, but he's an Invisible Man to this crowd.

Mike's Militia is going to change all of that. Be warned: my militia is no place for slackers or yuppies. There is no cappuccino and no NPR. You will have to meet people who are uneducated, crude, and like to go line-dancing. *You* may have to go line-dancing. Here are the requirements to join Mike's Militia:

1. You must be male or female.

2. You must count your birthday from the day you left your mother's womb, not from the day you were conceived.

3. You must be able to tell the difference between the Democratic and Republican parties ("little" or "none" are both acceptable answers).

4. You must be able to name more CEOs of Fortune 500 companies than characters on "Friends."

5. You must watch "Friends," "Baywatch," "Melrose Place," "Walker: Texas Ranger," and other mass forms of popular entertainment so you know what the people are tuned in to so you can tune in to them. No Sweet Honey and the Rock concerts for at least six months.

6. You must read *The Wall Street Journal, Fortune, Forbes,* the *Weekly Standard, New Republic,* and *American Spectator* so that you know what the enemy is up to—and so you can understand why what they write is so appealing to large numbers of Americans. You must listen to Rush Limbaugh at least once a week for the same reason.

7. You must listen to country music. It is the voice of the people. Whether it's Faith Hill singing about battered women or Garth Brooks singing about gay rights, it is ten times more progressive than anything you'll hear on a corporate rock station.

8. You must always carry an emergency quarter in your pocket. I don't know why, but I learned this in Boy Scouts and it seemed like a good idea at the time. Except then it was a dime.

9. You must know the Heimlich maneuver and perform it at least once a month.

10. You must avoid all foods labeled "Fat-Free." That is usually a lie; these foods contain so much sugar, chemicals, and carbohydrates that you will be way too sluggish to carry out your duties as a militia member.

• • •

Now that you've met the requirements, here's what we're going to do in Mike's Militia:

1. Take over the Democratic Party. We will take it over just like the Christian Coalition took over the Republican Party. This can be done if every militia member runs as a precinct delegate. We will then end up having a majority of our militia holding seats at the county conventions. Before they know what is happening to them, we'll be nominating *our* candidates. Until we accomplish this goal, we will sup-

port progressive third-party efforts (Labor Party, the Greens, New Party, etc.).

2. Descend on our state and national capitals to push for legislation to control Corporate America. No more getting rich at our expense.

3. Boycott all companies that downsize for profit, that do not promote women and minorities, that pollute the environment, and that have unsafe working conditions. No justice, no jingle-jangle at the cash register.

4. Open abortion clinics in the 80 percent of the country that no longer has them because they currently fear retaliation from Right to Life and Operation Rescue. Groups that harass women going in for an abortion will be harassed at their churches, their homes, their places of work, and wherever they go. They'll be given a taste of their own medicine and then we'll see how long they keep up their activities.

5. Volunteer to help organize workers into unions. Whenever a member visits a 7-Eleven, he or she will hand the clerk a card with this phone number on it: (800) 342-1235. This is the main number for the AFL-CIO (they've got a better guy in charge now), and they can direct the worker to a union organizer.

6. Get on cable access and produce a show with decent-quality cameras so it doesn't look like shit. Paper Tiger TV will help (phone: (212) 420-9045). Publicize the show. Make it entertaining. If you just sit there and lecture people, Militia Command will personally come and pull your plug.

7. Mike's Militia will have its own web site on the Internet and will actively use the World Wide Web to communicate with and organize others. If you abhor computers and/or the Internet—get over it. Corporate America has inadvertently given us an incredible tool to reach one another cheaply and quickly. Let's use it before they figure out a way to take it away from us! Contact us at the Michael Moore page http://www.randomhouse.com/

8. Militia Headquarters will make its previous covert

actions available on videotape. *Roger & Me* and *The Best of TV Nation* can be ordered from Dog Eat Dog Films, PO Box 831, Radio City Station, New York, New York 10101. Each tape will cost $19, check or money order only. All proceeds will go to stop the other militias—no profit will go to Mike from Michigan.

• • •

Here is a list of other resources to have in your local training camps:

- **Books**
  I don't read much, but I liked *Bury My Heart at Wounded Knee* when I read it back in the seventies. Also, any of the Spenser detective novels.

- **Magazines**
  The Nation, Harper's, The Progressive, In These Times, Multinational Monitor, Corporate Crime Reporter, Labor Notes, TV Guide . . . (hey, they put me in the crossword puzzle).

- **Home-Care Products**
  Furniture wax, stain remover sticks, lint rollers, Dirt Devil, baby wipes, air fresheners, and 2000 Flushes.

- **Movies to Rent (and watch with your date/spouse)**
  Lost in America, Monty Python's Life of Brian, Pee-Wee's Big Adventure, What's Up, Tiger Lily?, Gremlins 2, Clueless, Sherman's March, The People Under the Stairs, Melvin and Howard.

- **Movies to Rent (without your date/spouse)**
  A Clockwork Orange, Taxi Driver, American Dream, Hoop Dreams, Sophie's Choice, Lamerica, Do the Right Thing, Johnny Got His Gun, Salvador, American Job, The Emperor's Naked Army Marches On.

- **Good Places to Eat in Des Moines**
  China Wok, 223-8408; Gino's Restaurant and Lounge, 282-4029; Imperial Garden, 223-8441; Figlia's, 964-9011; Four Seasons Diner, 262-7692; Garcia's Mexican Restaurant, 270-0800; Jesse's Embers West, 225-9711; Tusi's Latin King Restaurant, 266-4466; Lonestar Steakhouse and Saloon, 223-9606; The Pier, 285-6996; Riccelli's Mainliner, 285-0401; Robin's Wood Oven Grill, 287-2080; Old Country Buffet, 285-4663; Saigon, 262-1928; Sbarro Italian Eatery, 225-9948; Seven Stars Greek & Middle Eastern Restaurant, 255-2560; Shoney's, 270-9616; Side Saddle Cafe, 282-7041; Ted's Coney Island, 243-8947; Village Inn Restaurant and Bakery, 223-0010; Waveland Cafe, 279-4341; Wings Bar and Grill, 287-6464; Yee Ho Garden, 285-8500; The Younkers Tearoom, 247-7161.

- **Good People to Know**
  I don't know many good people, but if you do let me know—I'll put them in the paperback edition.

• • •

There are maneuvers you are required to perform with this book. These include: pass it around, copy it, use it as a coaster, call Hollywood studios and tell them you *must* see the movie version of this book.

Members of Mike's Militia will know each other on the street by the Detroit Tigers baseball caps they are wearing. When you pass each other, tip your hat, repeat the secret mantra—"Gingrich Got Only 20 Percent!"—and continue on with your efforts to improve the country. If you encounter any opposition from executives in suits, especially those who seek to downsize you, you'll know what to tell them by the title of this book.

Downsized

Rightsized

Destaffed

Degrown

Dehired

Involuntarily separated

Personnel surplus reduction

Transitioned

Resource reallocation

A save (as in "savings" to the company)

Displaced

Dislocated

Disemployed

Redundancy elimination

Workforce imbalance correction

Fired

—from the pages of THE NEW YORK TIMES

EVERYONE FIRED
Wall Street Reacts Favorably

Dow Pushes Past 10,000

By JOE MORGANSTERNLY

The Dow Jones Industrial Average, continuing a trend it began in the early 1990s, finally broke through a barrier no one ever thought imaginable and closed the day up 3,900 points at 10,522. The average share rose an incredible $244. Traders on the floor of the New York Stock Exchange became delirious at the 4:00 P.M. closing bell, throwing anything into the air they could get their hands on.

"The Dow hitting 10,000! This is better than sex," exclaimed Miles Stanton of Bear Sterns. "I'm going out and buying a new boat!"

Others on Wall Street were more reflective.

"I was here back in '91 when the Dow broke 3,000," remarked Ben Vandenberg of Merrill Lynch. "We thought we had died and gone to heaven, that nothing could ever beat that day. And then it just kept going up, up, and up. But hitting 10,000? Somebody pinch me."

When the Market closed Friday, the Dow Jones was already at 6,687 and showing healthy gains for most · investors. But the tremendous surge that began this morning is believed to be in response to the news that every Fortune 500 company has fired all of their domestic employees effective immediately. Nearly 10 million American workers will lose their jobs, and Wall Street reacted favorably.

"It's a win-win situation," said Mickey Kantor, U.S. Secretary of Commerce and the man who negotiated the original NAFTA and GATT treaties and created a boom in moving American jobs overseas. "Literally hundreds of American shareholders have become instant millionaires. And millions of workers will now be able to pursue other activities."

Creative Thinking

The practice of Wall Street rewarding companies that fire workers en masse was initiated in 1993 when IBM announced it would cut 35,000 jobs. The following day, IBM's stock rose by three points. Suddenly, everyone was eager to announce massive firings, even if their companies were doing well and making a profit with their existing workers. It was simply the sheer bravado that the market seemed to appreciate.

"To eliminate 10,000 jobs at a drop of a hat," remarked Bill Boyton of First Boston, "became a way of saying, 'We're in charge here, and if you don't like it—*Hasta la vista!*'"

The success of this downsizing or "rightsizing"—and its financial rewards—apparently spurred this most recent development.

"Corporations are required to produce the largest dividend they can for their shareholders," said Ralph Mayfair, president of the Manufacturers Association of America. "If that means downsizing the workforce by 100 percent, then so be it."

Historic Day

The actions this weekend by General Electric, General Motors, IBM, Bristol Myers, RJR Nabisco, Unisys, Boeing, and others mark the largest single announcement of corporate layoffs in U.S. history. Bill Needham, head of communications at Sachs Goldman, cautioned against any overreaction.

"It would be wrong to portray this as a mass firing," Needham said. "Some management personnel in the front offices will retain their jobs, as will truckers and warehouse workers involved with receiving imports. We should guard against anyone who tries to turn this issue into one of class warfare. That could be very divisive."

It is expected that most of the products produced by these companies will now be built overseas.

A source at one of the corporations, who asked not to be identified, commented, "Our stockholders reacted favorably each time we would downsize about 10,000 employees. Then somebody said, 'Why not downsize the whole damn company?' It was one of those moments where everyone just looked at everyone else and we knew that we were in the presence of sheer genius."

New Opportunities

It is unclear whether the idea to get rid of everybody all at once was a coordinated effort among the participating companies, or whether it happened coincidentally. Whatever the maneuvering, the result was clear. Shareholders have tripled the wealth they possessed last Friday, CEOs have made millions in bonuses, and entire communities will thrive as popular ghost towns for tourists.

"That's our system," remarked a somewhat somber President Clinton. "We have to believe in the free market system. My heart goes out to those who have lost their jobs. I will continue to press forward to get the minimum wage raised to five dollars and forty cents an hour."

Jack Welch, chairman of General Electric, had more concrete advice for the downsized workers.

"We've got 40 openings at our Tijuana facility right now," beamed a jubilant Welch. "I'd be more than happy to accept applications from any of our U.S. workers who would like to relocate there. Just give our personnel department a call—and it will definitely help if you can speak Spanish!"

Acknowledgments

THIS IS MY FIRST BOOK. My parents taught me to write before I entered kindergarten, so my first thanks are to them. I'm very lucky to have such good parents.

I had incredible assistance in producing this book from four individuals who worked around the clock doing research, checking facts, and being a sounding board for the ideas I've expressed.

First and foremost is my wife, Kathleen Glynn. She was the de facto editor, tirelessly going over every page of the manuscript and cleaning it up so the rest of you could read it. Without her initial encouragement for me to write this book, it never would have happened. She, too, is from Flint, and our frequent trips back home always inspire us to keep doing what we're doing. I have promised her that, for the first time in my life, I'll dance in public if she'll just let someone publish *her* book.

Gillian Aldrich, perhaps the best coworker one could have, ran the office, ran the schedule, ran to FedEx at 8:59 P.M., and once got to go for a run in Central Park on that day we decided to all get healthy. We were back to our old habits the next day. Gillian also volunteered to allow her home address to be used as the headquarters for The John Wayne Gacey Fan Club and Satan Worshipers for Dole. She will now be bothered with junk mail from every lunatic group in the country for the rest of her life. For that, I am sorry.

Tia Lessin, who headed up the research, is a journalistic and political dynamo (she was also one of the key producers of Crackers, the Corporate Crime Chicken, on "TV Nation"). Tia was fearless in conducting interviews with the Secret Service and Right to Life. If, for any reason, I am not able to fulfill my duties, she will be named commander of Mike's Militia.

Joanne Doroshow, the woman who was in charge of all the research on "TV Nation" (not to mention leading the legal fight against Three Mile Island a few years ago), went over every word in this book to make sure the facts were correct and the spirit true. She's also a lawyer, so she's got a file cabinet full of documents to back up what you've read on these pages. Joanne is one of the most honest people I know and, best of all, she plays her rock and roll *real loud.*

My sister Veronica devoted many days to this book, searching the Internet for the information I needed and being her usual loving, supportive sisterly self. Also, my thanks to her daughter Kelsey, for making the calls to Republican voters none of us wanted to talk to, and to her sister Leah for playing catch with me.

We also had a great deal of assistance from two hardworking interns who were there for us whenever we needed them—Beth Kotler and Michael Skolnick. Volunteers from Columbia University's journalism program, including Paula Murphy, Molly Ginty, and Kurt Gottshalk, were very helpful.

Thanks also to my sister-in-law Dolores Glynn, who took the photo of the Flint factory while it was being demolished. She is always there for us when we need a touch of reality and a laugh from back home.

I cannot sing enough the praises of Crown Publishers and Random House, so I won't. Actually, I can't really sing. But let me express my deepest appreciation to Ann Patty, my editor at Crown, for convincing everybody there that the republic could fall without this book. Every now and then you run into one of the "good people" in this world, and Ann is one of them. Karen Rinaldi was the editor "on the front lines" for this book, and it's because of her enthusiasm that this project was finished on time and in English. (She still thinks O.J. did it.)

The entire staff at Crown (Whitney Cookman, Lauren Dong, Camille Smith, Jane Searle, Andy Martin, Tina Constable, Hilary Bass, Brian Belfiglio, the relentless sales force) and its owner, Random House, and its owner, Advance Publications, and *its* owners, the Newhouse family (hey, where's the chapter on *this* conglomerate!), have been among the most accommodating and respectful group of people I have ever worked with. The bossman at Crown, Chip Gibson, is such a cool guy, *he* should be running General Motors.

I walked into Andrew Wylie's office eight years ago and told him I wanted to write a book. Andrew, the Bad Boy of literary agents, said he'd do anything for me. But I got distracted making a couple of films and TV shows. When I returned in 1996 with the idea for this book, he flew into action and found the right publisher. Bridget Love at Andrew's agency was also very helpful.

Thanks also to Ken Starr, Barry Hersh, David Tenzer, and Robert Bookman for making sure *I* don't get downsized.

A number of individuals and organizations, who spend their lives working for little credit and no money to make America a better place, deserve a heap of thanks for providing me with crucial information in this book. They are: Dave Yettaw, past president of U.A.W. local 599 and a leader in the New Directions union dissident movement; Russell Mokhiber and his *Corporate Crime Reporter;* John Richard and all the people who toil away in Ralph Nader's office, including Janice Shields of the Corporate Welfare Project; all the people at FAIR (Fairness and Accuracy in Reporting) who put out the media watchdog newsletter *Extra!;* Gary Brouse at the Interfaith Center on Corporate Responsibility; the Council on Economic Priorities; Christian Parenti for his research on prisons; Nathan Callahan and his book on Bob Dornan (*Shut Up, Fag!*); the Alternatives Federal Credit Union in Ithaca, New York, for letting us set up strange checking accounts (Abortionists for Buchanan, etc.); Judy Marks at the National Immigration Forum; *The Nation* and *Harper's* magazines; and Rodney Walker in Congressman John Conyers's office, who was always there whenever we needed the inside scoop on the federal government.

Finally, on a personal level, I want to point out that none of us come to the places in our lives that we're at without the help and guidance and comradery of others. Whatever political conclusions I've arrived at here are the result of having known a number of good people back in Flint, and I would like to acknowledge the spark they provided that eventually led to this book.

First and foremost is my cousin, Pat Simons, who came to

Michigan from New York City every summer when we were kids and opened our eyes to a world outside of Flint.

My friends Al Hirvela, Rod Birleson, Bob Wilhelm, and Ben Hamper continue to be a valuable source of inspiration, ideas, and support. Much of this book comes from a lot of late-night "shootin' the shit," driving with them and Kathleen around Buick City.

Others who had a significant impact in my "formative years" include Jack Stanzler, Laurie White, Gary Wood, Phyllis Valdez, Mary Hail, Dave Hall, Sam Riddle, Kenny Siegel, Harold Ford, Barry and Cyndi Wolf, Jeff Gibbs, Peter Cavanaugh, Gary Boren, Doris Suciu, Fr. Dick Preston, Doug Cunningham, Dan Bremer, Tom Scott, Bob Collins, Jan Kittel, Ralph Arellano, Bobby Crim and his sons, and many, many others, including my sister Anne, who went with me on our first antiwar demonstration to Washington, D.C., when we were teenagers.

Also, thanks to those teachers who encouraged me at an early age to question what was going on and write it down: Thelma Clay, Craig Hardy, Mary Biagini, Marty Trepus, Dave Wood, Gary Hale, John Tempia, and, of course, the Sisters of St. Joseph, who made sure I could construct a sentence—or else! Please don't hold any of my grammatical mistakes against them; they did their best considering who (ouch! I mean "whom") they had to teach.

Finally, I want to thank my daughter, Natalie Rose. She is the real writer of the family. Natalie has pages of hilarious stuff that I should have grabbed and published in this book, but she somehow got the landlord to put a lock on her desk. Her and her mother's wonderful sense of humor and capacity for pity is the only reason I get to come home at night.

About the Author

MICHAEL MOORE is the award-winning director of the groundbreaking documentary *Roger & Me,* which became the largest-grossing nonfiction film of all time. He is the creater and host of "TV Nation," which won the Emmy Award in 1995. His other films include *Canadian Bacon* (an official selection of the 1995 Cannes International Film Festival) and *Pets or Meat: The Return of Flint.* He was also the editor of the *Flint Voice/Michigan Voice* and one of the first eighteen-year-olds elected to public office in this country. He has been an answer on both "Jeopardy!" *and* "Wheel of Fortune." His most recent book was the hugely successful *Stupid White Men.*

Michael Moore lives in New York City with his wife, Kathleen Glynn, and daughter, Natalie Rose. He can be reached at PO Box 831, Radio City Station, New York, New York 10101-0831, or at MMFlint@aol.com.